Dollar Default

∞

How the Federal Reserve and Government Betrayed Your Trust

∞

Bill Cross

Consulting Editor: Hazel Cross

Copyright © 2012 Bill Cross

All rights reserved. No portion of this book may be reproduced, stored in a retrieval system or transmitted in any form or by any means – electronic, mechanical, photocopy, recording, scanning, or other – except for brief quotations in critical reviews or articles, without the prior written permission of the publisher.

ISBN: 13: 978-1475261080
ISBN-10: 147526108X

Dedication

Dollar Default is dedicated to my wife and daughter, Hazel and Molly Margaret. They are the love of my life. I also would like to thank my parents Betty Jo and Bill Cross. They are the biggest cheerleaders a son could ever hope for.

Default

Default is the failure to meet the financial terms of a contract. It is the breach of a covenant. In 1933 the United States government broke a covenant with the people of the United States when it ended her pledge to exchange dollars for gold on demand. In 1968 the United States government broke a covenant with the people to redeem silver certificates for silver bullion. In 1971 the United States government broke a covenant with her international trading partners to redeem dollars for gold as promised. These are dollar defaults.

Table of Contents

Acknowledgements: i
Time Line: ii
Preface: vi

Chapter 1: A Brief History of Gold and Silver: *1*

Chapter 2: Paper Money Gains a Foothold: *15*

Chapter 3: The Continental: Hell's Half Acre: *31*

Chapter 4: The Constitutional Dollar: 1792-2012: *41*

Chapter 5: Origin of the Federal Reserve: *60*

Chapter 6: 1933*: 78*

Chapter 7: Bretton Woods and the Nixon Shock: *105*

Chapter 8: Concluding Remarks: *117*

Bibliography: *132*
Appendix: FDR Proclamations, EO's, Fireside Chats: 136
Index: 172
About the Author: 174

The Dollar and The Coin

"The unit or dollar is a known coin, and the most familiar of all to the mind of the public. It is already adopted from South to North, has identified our currency, and therefore happily offers itself a unit already introduced."

Thomas Jefferson

This begs the question: *If a dollar is a coin, what is the coin?*

Acknowledgements

The words in this book rely extensively on the research and scholarship of other historians. Readers of these pages will recognize the names of many of these scholars in the bibliography and footnotes. I do not know any of these scholars other than reading their works or seeing them on television. Hopefully, I have represented their views accurately. If not, the fault lies exclusively with me. In addition to my wife, daughter and parents this book is dedicated to these scholars and others unmentioned who put me on the path of discovery on the topics in this book.

Monetary Time Line

600–700 B.C.: Private merchants in Lydia create earliest known coins in western world. Made of electrum, a combination of gold, silver and copper.

300–400 B.C.: High quality Greek gold and silver coinage introduced.

300 B.C.: Roman coinage begins.

200 B.C.: Roman silver Denarius introduced.

100 B.C.: Roman gold Aureus introduced.

301 A.D.: Roman gold Solidus introduced.

1252: Firenze gold florin introduced.

1489: British gold sovereign introduced.

1526–1604: Establishment of Spanish, French and English colonies in America from Maine to Florida. Most fail.

1526–1690: Period of commodity medium of exchange in America. Wampum, deer skins, beaver pelts, tobacco, corn, and rice are common mediums. Gold and silver coins rare, but increase over time.

1550: Spanish silver and gold mining begins in New World.

1606: Jamestown founded.

1620: Pilgrims arrive in America.

1652–1684: First silver mint in America. Closed by Charles II.

1690: The Massachusetts Bay Colony starts first experiment with paper money.

Timeline

1690–1775: Government paper money experiments surge in colonies. Most end in disaster. Free market selects Spanish milled silver dollar as preferred medium of exchange.

1704: English Queen Anne Proclamation establishing fixed proportions of silver and gold coins according to "assays" and weight. Cites Spanish milled silver dollar as leading coin which does "usually pass in payment" in colonies.

1775–1782: Continental paper money in America during Revolution. Ends disastrously. Drives gold and silver out of circulation.

1787: Constitutional Convention.

1792: Dollar defined in terms of silver. Silver defined in terms of gold. Gold defines dollar.

1792–1933: Long period of price stability except during war.

1792-1834: Silver period in the United States. Silver used widely. Gold rarely used. Gresham's Law.

1794: American silver dollar introduced.

1795: Gold American Eagle introduced.

1812, War of: Mid Atlantic banks issue paper money. New England banks resist.

1853-1879: Gold period. Gold widely used. Silver exported east to India.

1862–1879: Period of the greenback. Gold redemption payments suspended during civil war. Prices double.

1873: Crime of 1873. Silver demonetized.

1879-1914: High moment of gold standard.

Timeline

1900: Gold Standard Act in United States confirms de facto gold standard already in existence.

1907, Panic of: Leads to formation of commission to reform banking system.

1913: Federal Reserve Act passed. Dollar loses over 95% of its purchasing power over next century from money printing.

1914: World War I starts. Major Powers except United States exit gold standard.

1915–1925 Period of paper money.

1917: United States enters World War I. Suspends international export of gold.

1919–1935 Purchasing power of gold ranges from lowest point to highest point in world history to date.

1926–1931: Gold Exchange Standard. Britain pegs to gold at pre-World War I level despite massive debt accumulation from war. Deflationary move in overall context. United States helps Britain with loose monetary policy to offset British loss of gold.

1931–1945: Britain exits gold exchange standard. Free floating paper currencies against each other, not gold.

1933, March 9: Emergency Banking Act. FDR seizes people's gold at $20.67. Once has people's gold FDR revalues dollar downward to $35 per gold ounce. Owning gold made illegal for citizens. Fine and jail if disobey.

1944-1971: Bretton Woods Treaty. Dollar becomes world reserve currency. United States agrees to exchange dollars for gold from trade imbalances on demand. Many countries jump at the opportunity as debt and deficits accumulate in the United States. USA gold reserves plummet during the period.

Timeline

1960–1968: London Gold Pool. Central banks suppress price of gold to maintain $35 peg to dollar. Size and scope of government increasing. Deficits and inflation building.

1965, Coinage Act of: Silver content reduced or removed from coins.

1968: Silver certificates can no longer be exchanged for bullion. Gold backing for currency stopped.

1971: Nixon shock closes the gold window. Foreign countries no longer can exchange dollars for gold from trade imbalances. Paper money currencies trade against each other rather than gold. United States essentially declares bankruptcy with the move.

1971–1973: Smithsonian Agreement among nations pegs currencies to the dollar versus gold at fixed exchange rate. Fails in fourteen months.

1975: Legal again for United States citizens to own gold.

1971–2012: Greatest accumulation of debt in history of the world in United States without discipline of gold standard on policy makers. Dollar plummets against the currencies of its trading partners. Cost of living skyrockets.

1999–2002: Britain sells 395 tons of gold at 20 year lows.

2009: Gold breaks above $1000.

2000–2012: Gold climbs steadily to roughly $1900 / ounce.

Preface

Dollar Default traces the history of the development of money in the United States. It tells the story of the various mediums of exchange used in America from the earliest settlements in colonial times through modern day.

The major emphasis in *Dollar Default* is 1) to discuss the early forms of money 2) tell the story of how money in the United States has evolved 3) discuss constitutional money as defined in the United States Constitution 4) reveal the sordid details of how money in America evolved from a paper money system to Constitutional money and back again to a paper money system the framers reviled, detested and eradicated from the American arrangement of money 5) explain how the people of the United States lost their right to redeem their currency for silver and gold on demand.

This book specifically targets the breaking of the silver and gold covenant with the American people by representatives of the United States government and big banks during the 20th Century. *Dollar Default* is a modest and humble attempt to enlighten the reader the extent to which the United States government has drifted from a clear constitutional principle of money. It is a reminder of what once was, but no longer is.

The reader of *Dollar Default* will gain keen insight into why the founders specifically legislated and defined the dollar in terms of silver and gold. You will learn the context of the times which led to this decision. The purpose of the book is to provide easily understood, tangible, vivid, real world reasons why the founders did what they did to define the dollar in terms of silver and gold. *Dollar Default* will discuss in broad, sweeping fashion how the heirs to sound money took the low road back to paper money, which is the exact opposite of what the founders designed based on their own real life experiences. As will be shown, their wisdom was well founded. The framers knew exactly what they

Preface

were doing. The question that will be answered is why did the heirs to sound constitutional money do what they did? Another question to be answered in *Dollar Default* is who were the beneficiaries of this revolutionary change from the intentions of the founders? A third question to be answered is who suffers and pays for the change?

Why did I write *Dollar Default*? Having followed things financial for some thirty years in my career I thought it prudent to write an orderly account of the monetary history of the United States for you, dear reader, so that you can have a solid foundation of your history. There's a lot of false history and propaganda being directed at the American people. The American people are being manipulated by the paper money vested interests. These people do not want you to know how far the moneyed interests, bankers and financial custodians of our legacy have drifted from the intentions of the founding fathers of the United States. Thus, I thought it wise to write a short treatise for you to read and have as a convenient reference.

Like so many others I too am distressed at the ever dwindling purchasing power of the paper money in my wallet. Fortunately, I took a few easy action steps that have lessened the pain, although not entirely. Indeed, my thirty years' time spent on "Wall Street" was not totally wasted. After reading *Dollar Default* it is my hope you will walk away with some insight and take action to protect you and your family's wealth based on the learning's of those who have gone before you.

When you read *Dollar Default* please do so from a 30,000 feet perspective. Look at the events from a long term viewpoint, and try to avoid the snare of getting embroiled in minutia. *Dollar Default* does not pretend to cover every financial incident or concept that has existed in America since 1600. Rather, the vision of the book is to give you an enriched understanding of the history of the dollar, paper money, gold and silver in American history: the big picture.

Preface

Upon completing a reading of *Dollar Default* you will have a better appreciation of the perils of paper money. This will arm you with information needed to know exactly what action steps to take to avoid the errors of those who preceded you. Insofar as you take action, you will be able to sleep a little easier at night. In addition, you will have the tools available to recognize immediately the sharks and charlatans who walk amongst us in the financial media. Last but not least, you will be reacquainted with the truth about American financial history, and the vision of the framers on money.

Initially, I intended to write *Dollar Default* for the segment of the American population who have a working knowledge of American financial history but would like to know more on the subject. But upon talking to literally hundreds of people about the topic of constitutional money I realized that *Dollar Default* was a subject that would benefit all Americans. The fact is that hardly anyone (actually no one) that I queried knew the definition of what a dollar was, including me before I started studying the issue. Furthermore, the people I spoke with ranged the gamut of the bell curve, both educationally and economically. Even legal experts were bewildered. So insofar as the paper moneyed interests wish to keep us uneducated on the subject of constitutional money one must admit they've accomplished their goal.

True, the dollar and the gold standard have been discussed hotly since the fateful days of default in 1933 and 1971. But the financial media and vested interests continue to portray all those who refuse to drink the Kool-Aid as fringe kooks who don't deserve to be taken seriously. Thus, much of what I write has faded into history. As a country we've developed something of a normalcy bias if not a collective Stockholm Syndrome when it comes to paper money. There are many reasons for this. The key beneficiaries of an irredeemable paper money would rather the public not know the past. The goal of this book is to fill in the missing pieces.

Preface

The format of the book will be simple. Since aiming at a wide audience technical and academic terms will be avoided to the maximum extent possible. Where appropriate an explanation of commonly used academic terms will be explained. References will be given for quotes. Bibliography is cited for the reader should they want a deeper reading and understanding. Footnotes will be cited at the bottom of each page for ease of use. They are provided mainly for the reader to pursue if choosing to get more detail than is necessary to make the main point clear. At the end of each chapter I will summarize the chapter and cite a few words that I think describe the key themes of the topic. I think this is a good way for people to remember a subject for future reference or discussion.

On a personal level, writing *Dollar Default* was a thorough delight. The time I spent crafting the project has helped me in a myriad of ways. It was a complete pleasure to get acquainted with the financial thinking of the likes of Thomas Jefferson, George Washington and Alexander Hamilton. Of course, as a Stockbroker, Investment Consultant and Money Manager I had a decent knowledge of some of the history of paper money and gold in the history of the United States and the world. But I got that information by reading in my spare time. I certainly did not receive any history on the topic of bimetallism or the gold standard either in undergraduate or graduate school while studying finance. It was as if silver and gold had never been used as money at any point in history. So I made it a point to do something about it insofar as my limited scope is able to do so. I have no illusions. But if the minds of just a few readers are impacted positively then the effort to write *Dollar Default* will have served its purpose.

It took a couple of years to research and write *Dollar Default*. To organize my thoughts I read important books written by Ron Paul, Murray Rothbard, Henry Hazlitt, Ferdinand Lips and Amity Shlaes and so on and so forth. You can find a list of some of the authors of the books I read in the Bibliography section at the back of the book. Their works are exceptional and my personal

Preface

education from their research was eye opening. All of my writings are attributable to these scholars. What I have attempted to do is organize a mountain of historical financial information written by experts in the field into a short, easily readable format.

What really captivated me in my research was the information I learned about the human effects a hyperinflationary, devalued paper money has on the people forced to use it. You'll find a flavor of the effects a devalued paper money has on people in the book. Sure, I knew about Weimar paper money in Germany after World War I. But, that wasn't American history. It never happened here, or did it?

Research opened my eyes otherwise. The facts I learned were sobering. In *Dollar Default* I have merged the details of these historical events into this book for your education. Hopefully, I have painted a clear picture of the nasty side-effects and unintended consequences of paper money for visual and hands on learners like me.

Dollar Default has been divided into easily digestible chapters. Each chapter deals with a separate but important topic. Each chapter focuses on a key theme that needs to be studied to understand American financial history. These themes are paper money, bimetallism, silver, gold, and the history of money in the United States, the gold coin standard, the Federal Reserve, the banking crisis of the Great Depression, Bretton Woods and the Nixon shock. I have done the best I can to make *Dollar Default* a quick, fun read. I hope you will agree. In any event, once completing a read of *Dollar Default* you will be armed with the lion's share of knowledge of American financial history, and why we are in the bind we are in today.

That said, my intention has been to stay loyal to the main topic in each chapter. Believe me, there is so much information surrounding each chapter topic that it was easy to careen off subject and into a briar patch of related but important points. But

Preface

while important to the topic a discussion of them would have added tremendous length to the book. So to the maximum extent possible I have bid to stay focused on the chapter topics to keep the book short and digestible, while providing context and background to the subject. Once again, *Dollar Default* makes no pretention to be an exhaustive study of the issues discussed. Yet it is my hope you will find value in the following pages.

Bill Cross
Houston, Texas
May, 2012

The hideous paper money tyrant knows who you are. He plans your capture and enslavement.

Chapter 1

A Brief History of Gold and Silver

Article 1, Section 8

Article 1, Section 8 of the United States Constitution gives Congress the right to "To coin Money, regulate the Value thereof, and of foreign Coin, and fix the Standard of Weights and Measures."

The Constitution of the United States gives Congress the right to coin and regulate money. Yet the Constitution is silent on the value, weights and measures of the coin. After ratification of the Constitution by the several states further legislation was needed to express the specifics. This was completed upon passage of the Coinage Act, or the Mint Act as it is sometimes called. The Coinage Act was passed by Congress on April 2, 1792. It established the United States Mint and regulated the coinage of the United States. This act defined the dollar in terms of silver, and defined silver in terms of gold as the unit of money in the United States. In addition, the Coinage Act declared gold and silver to be lawful tender and created a decimal system for American currency.

But why did the framers draft legislation and Congress enact into law a medium of exchange defined in terms of silver and gold coin? The answer is that the framers were well versed in the history of money. They knew what had worked in the past and what didn't. When they had a chance to create the best system that history had rendered they acted decisively and without hesitation. What the framers created was in exact contravention of the failed paper money system that existed at the time. Let's explore what prompted the founders to act as they did when they ratified the Constitution in 1787.

Mediums of Exchange

Gold and silver throughout history have been used as money. Both are mediums of exchange that man has used for over 2500 years to transact business. The reason for gold and silver money is that man understands the intrinsic value in both metals. Man understands the difficulty of finding gold and silver, digging it out of the ground, transporting it, and minting it into a distinguishable form for commerce. It's not easy. Mining is a hard business. Gold and silver are rare in nature. The ancient Greeks used gold and silver coins. The Romans did too. And so did early Americans. In each case the people in these civilizations used the value in the coin to determine what and how much of a particular good or service was worth to them in exchange for parting with their gold or silver.

It's hard to dispute the case against gold and silver as a medium of exchange. The free market chose gold and silver as the medium. Indeed, people fashioned metallic money across different civilizations and time lines.

Aristotle defined money in terms of divisibility, portability, durability and scarcity among certain other intrinsic qualities. Gold and silver meet these standards. Oil doesn't. Nor does land, or wheat, although at any given point in time one may find it necessary to use bread as money in a life-threatening situation. History is replete with examples of civilizations that voluntarily chose gold and silver as their medium of exchange. Studying history I have yet to discover a civilization where the people on their own accord chose paper money as their medium. It was the state and their closely affiliated cronies who for power, personal gain and influence forced paper money on the people. In other cases it was the state that introduced an illegitimate system of paper money to finance wars and other social causes,

Gold and Silver Characteristics

An examination of history proves man's affection for gold and silver. Gold has been the definitive representation of affluence, authority, power, splendor and stature for thousands of years. Both gold and silver have been used for industrial applications, money, jewelry, art and ornamentation. Gold and silver have excellent thermal and electrical capabilities. Both are found in the earth in relatively pure form. They're durable and resilient to the point of indestructability; they're malleable and beautiful in color and shine.

History has shown that where gold and silver have been the standard commercial medium that society has exhibited prosperity, national advancement, social improvement, cultural enhancement and governmental stability. Most importantly, gold and silver are key components of individual liberty and freedom. The gold and silver holder is a free man. He has protection from inflation and devaluation of paper money. He can carry his gold and silver with him anywhere in the world he travels and have a readily available, marketable and recognizable form of money as a medium of exchange.

With a timeline of 2500 years confirming its validation several conclusions can be drawn from gold and silver money. Studies have shown that the price of gold and silver fluctuate in the short term, sometimes wildly. Yet, holding fine gold and silver over the long term shields the holder from inflation of products and services as well as the frequent debasement of the coins by governments. The result is that the holder of gold and silver maintains his purchasing power in times of inflation, deflation and periods of crisis. Thus, the utility of gold and silver has stood the test of time.

The Lydians

According to Herodotus, a 5th century Greek historian, the Lydians, who lived in modern day western Turkey, were the first civilization to use gold and silver coins.[1] The Egyptians had been mining gold since around 4000 B.C. However, the Egyptians did not use gold for money. Mostly the Egyptians used gold for funerary masks, jewelry, statues of gods and royal chariots. It was the Lydians that began to use gold and silver coins - actually electrum, a naturally occurring amalgam of gold, silver, copper and trace metals - as money in exchange for food, materials, supplies and the like in the first retail shops. The coins were a pale yellow or a bright yellow depending on the amount of gold in each coin. The use of these coins originated around 650 B.C.

As soon as these coins became accepted mediums of exchange their usage swiftly began to spread throughout the region. Improvements in refining techniques quickly emerged. The gold, silver and copper components of electrum were separated. This allowed for the smelting of

---

[1] The History of Herodotus, Volume 1 (New York: E.P. Dutton and Company, 1916) p. 50.

pure gold, silver and small denomination copper coins. With the advent of pure silver and gold coins, trade and industrial progress began to increase significantly, the result of a more efficient and common medium of exchange. The Lydian monarch Croesus generally is credited with striking the first pure gold coins. Croesus ruled Lydia from 560 B.C. to 547 B.C. At the end of his rule Croesus' army was defeated by the Persians who immediately adopted the gold coin as their own after hauling most if not all of the gold of Lydia back to Persia. Croesus' name throughout history has been a symbol of great wealth, especially in Persia.

The Greeks

Coinage in the Greek world began around the same time as it did in the age of the Lydians. Historians generally ascribe Greek mercenaries to bringing the first gold (electrum) coins to Greece from Lydia. Coincidently, a booming free enterprise system took hold in Greece. This was during the 4th and 3rd centuries B.C. By the time of Alexander the Great, gold and silver coins had reached a very high form of artistic beauty. More than half of the two thousand or so Greek city states issued their own gold and silver coins.

Tutored by Aristotle until the age of 16, Alexander the Great by virtue of his military campaigns spread the practice of gold and silver coin commerce. Alexander's campaigns extended from the Adriatic Sea to the Indus River area in modern Pakistan, India and Afghanistan. Part and parcel of Alexander's campaigns was the minting of new money plundered from captured booty, particularly from the Persians as payback from the defeat of Croesus some two centuries earlier. It is estimated that Alexander carted off some 10,000 tons of gold and silver from the Persian cities of Persepolis, Susa and Ecbatana.[2] This fantastic treasure of wealth was circulated throughout the civilized parts of the world of the period. Thereupon, Greek merchants and traders filtered into the areas conquered by Alexander and further spread the practice of gold and silver coin commerce. The time period of Alexander's campaigns spanned from roughly 334 B.C. until his death in 323 B.C.

As it happened, Greek economic dominance began to steadily diminish due to a continuous series of wars in which the city states were embroiled. All efforts were made to stop the decline. But incessant wars, the destruction of property, the loss of lives and the bondage of people into slavery created too big an obstacle for a once thriving economy to overcome. More and more the Greek city states found themselves too preoccupied with preparations for war and defense to properly focus on the private economy. Too much emphasis was placed on erecting armies, navies and procuring the latest military inventions. Soon wholesale nationalization of the economy took place in a devastating blow to private enterprise.

To pay for the wars the Greeks did as most all governments that followed would do: they debased their gold and silver coins rather than raise taxes on the people. This the Greeks did slowly over time until eventually only copper coins circulated. Basically, this was the end of Greek ascendency in the ancient world. With worthless money, a devastated economy and bitter strife within the realm the Greeks were supplanted in due course by the Romans.

---

[2] The United States has about 8000 tons of gold bullion in 2012.

A Brief History of Gold and Silver

The Romans

Around 300 B.C. the Romans introduced coinage to the realm as their traders and merchants began to rub elbows with the Greeks in commerce. The Romans quickly embraced the concept of coins as a medium of exchange. As trade and commerce grew the Romans took steps to integrate their coinage with the Greeks. Employing Greek artisans the Romans designed their coins in a fashion closely aligned with that of Greek coinage using specifications familiar to the Greeks. These steps fostered trust and common conventions. The result was vastly improved trade which lasted for several hundred years.

Over time the Romans developed four different mining methodologies: simple river panning, surface mining, hydraulic mining and deep vein mining. In the Las Medulas region of Spain the Romans built enormous mining operations employing seven 60 mile long aqueduct systems to wash gold from the soil.[3] Eventually, the Romans would import from Spain some 1400 tons of gold per year.

Among other sites, deep mines were dug centuries later in the Ogafau region of Wales after the invasion of Britain. Although coinage was the primary purpose of the mining, the rich in the Roman domain wore gold as a status symbol. Later, with the accepted medium of coins as money, Roman generals were conferred the right by the Senate to mint coins to pay their soldiers. Maybe because of its beauty, high value and relative rarity among common citizens, the Roman commoners did not use gold coins, known as the Aureus, for day to day business transactions. For these latter, the Romans

---

[3] Martin Goodman, Rome and Jerusalem: The Clash of Ancient Civilizations (New York, Alfred A. Knopf, 2007), page 93.

used the silver Denarius valued at twenty five to one per Aureus. The Denarius was introduced in 211 B.C., although there were earlier silver coins of Denarius type persuasion. The Aureus was introduced in the first century B.C.

Eventually the Romans displaced the Greeks as the dominant power in Europe, the Mediterranean, North Africa and Asia Minor. Roman wealth was unsurpassed in its day. Hundreds of millions of gold and silver coins were struck and circulated throughout the Roman age. However, for many reasons the Roman Empire began to recede. Possibly to pay for his building projects after the great fire in Rome in 64 A.D., or maybe because of shortage of metal, Nero began to debase the coins. Debasement continued for several centuries until the coins became worthless with but trifling amounts of metal purity composed mostly of copper.

The Byzantines

As the Roman Empire began to wind down in the west another Roman empire took root in the east. Centered in Constantinople, known originally as New Rome but later as Byzantium, this empire lasted roughly 1000 years beyond the collapse of the Western Roman Empire as it came to be known. Constantinople, the hub of the Eastern Roman Empire, became the largest and wealthiest city during Middle Age period. The Byzantines expanded the use of the gold Solidus introduced by Diocletian in 301 A.D. in the Western Roman Empire. In time the Solidus replaced the Aureus as the Roman gold coin.

The Solidus gold coin, or Nomisma as it was called in Byzantium[4], was recognized for its purity. The horrible

---

[4] The 'Solidus' was called the 'Bezant' outside the empire.

experience of debasement and decline in the Western Empire was a well-known fact. For this reason the Byzantines were sticklers for maintaining the gold purity of the Solidus. For roughly 700 years the precise weight and purity of the Solidus was maintained by repeatedly melting down the gold content and reissuing the coin after it was reclaimed by the treasury as payment for taxes.

Because of high standards and purity, widespread acceptance of the Solidus soon became the norm among traders and merchants despite the fact that the Byzantines forbade the use of it outside the realm of the empire. Arab merchants trading with the Romans readily accepted the Solidus alongside their own gold Dinar which had come to prominence in North Africa and the Middle East with the rise of Islam.

Perhaps by coincidence, but maybe not, the Byzantine Empire began to fray at the edges in the 11th century. This was about the time gold coin debasement began in Byzantium. The main causes for debasement were fiscal burdens brought on by clashes with the Islamic caliphate, military discontent, coup d'états and church-state battles. Once the slippery slope of debasement gained steam confidence and trust were broken permanently. The debasement started in earnest in 1030 and by the time of 1080 the gold content of the Solidus was almost non-existent.

War and conflict were the main culprits for the debasement. In 1071 the Byzantines were decisively defeated in the Battle of Manzikert in eastern Turkey. The loss was the turning point for Byzantium and one from which she never really recovered. More and more expenditures were required to pay for defense of an ever decreasing realm. This development extrapolated into fewer sources of manpower and food for the empire. Attempts were made to arrest the situation. Church gold and silver was seized, and loyal Romans turned in their own private reserves. In the meantime, a new super-refined gold coin, the Hyperpryon, was introduced in 1092 to offset the calamity. But it too was subject to debasement. As events unfolded, the Eastern Roman Empire was pressed back into the gates of Constantinople to the point where it was but a shell of its former self. In the end Constantinople was captured by Mehmet II in 1453.[5]

The Italian City States

After the fall of the Western Roman Empire, city states began to spring up in the old western empire around the 1000's. These included modern day Florence, Genoa, Venice, Pisa and Milan. With prosperity, or maybe because of it, gold and silver came into prominent use among the merchant class. Among the most popular gold coins issued were the Florentine gold Fiorino d'oro (the Florin) and the Venetian Ducat, although all the other city states minted their own gold coins, too.

By no coincidence a stable gold medium of exchange ushered in a great era of commercial and trade success for the city states of the old Western Roman Empire. Owing to their great wealth the small city states of northern Italy were prime targets for foreign invaders eager to plunder their vast wealth. This was a constant problem. In any event, the rise of prosperity of these city states and the eventual rollback of

---

[5] Roger Crowley, 1453: The Holy War for Constantinople and The Clash of Islam and The West (New York: Hyperion, 2005), 25-26.

Arabic conquest generally is attributed to the advent of the renaissance, a period in which the arts, literature, music, and science thrived in Western Europe.

The Britons

Britain has a long tradition of using gold and silver coins for trade. Digs have unearthed Greek, French and Roman gold and silver coins. The first gold coins the Britons minted were around 150 B.C. The prototype of their first coins were the ones then existing in Gaul, which had been modeled on the ones created by Philip of Macedon, the father of Alexander the Great. The Britons got the idea for gold coin commerce either through contact in trade with the Phoenicians or through cross channel trade with Gaul.[6]

In the mid first century the Romans invaded and conquered Britain. Thereupon they introduced their own conventions and customs. By the end of the first century almost all the coins in Britain were Roman. This lasted until around 450 A.D. when the Romans withdrew. Predictably, the Romans took most of the coinage with them. Barter thus returned to Britain until the mid-600 timeframe when the Anglo-Saxons, after conquering the island, introduced their own brand of gold and silver coins. Over the next few centuries various types of coins were introduced depending on who was in power at the time.

The year 1489 brought political and economic stability to Britain. It was then that the English gold sovereign was first issued during the reign of Henry VII after an extended

---

[6] Edwin Walter Kemmerer, Gold and the Gold Standard: The Story of Gold Money, Past Present and Future (New York and London: McGraw-Hill Book Company, 1944), pp. 26-27.

period of political intrigue and wars.[7] In one form or other British sovereign gold coins have been minted until the present day.

Summary

Gold and silver became money through the choice of the free market.

A few conclusions can be drawn from the history of gold over the millennia. Gold initially was worn as jewelry or an adornment in the early stages of Egyptian civilization. Gold was owned for its beautiful characteristics, shine and color.

Over time gold converted to money and was used in the minting of coins. Basically, there are only a handful of gold coins that have circulated in the western world for the past two thousand years: the Roman Aureus, the Roman Solidus, the Arab Dinar, the Venetian Ducat and the British Sovereign.

The day to day use of silver coins in world history is much more common than that of gold coins. Since the earliest of times silver has been dug, smelted and minted into coins the world over. Silver coins are considered the first and most common form of mass coinage in the world.

Throughout history the price per ounce of gold has been significantly more expensive than silver. As such people have tended to use silver coins for their daily transactions except in a few time periods. The period during the California gold rush in the United States comes to mind.

---

[7] The Wars of the Roses was fought from 1455 to 1485.

A Brief History of Gold and Silver

During this period the price of gold relative to silver on a historical basis prompted people to use gold over silver.

Although there are too many to name, the Greek drachma, the Roman denarius and the Spanish milled silver dollar are three of the most widely used silver coins in world history.

There are many examples in the history of the world of gold and silver coin debasement. Here is one example. From the time of Nero's first steps at debasement in 64 A.D. until the fall of the Western Roman Empire in 476 A.D. the price of wheat rose about one million percent against the ever decreasing Roman money. Amazingly, the coin debasement was only about 4% on average per year.

For comparison, since the Federal Reserve was formed in the United States in 1914, the dollar has been devalued and debased over ninety-five percent, or about 3.4% per year. Using the Bureau of Labor Statistics website the purchasing power of $1 in 1914 requires spending $22.70 in 2012. This represents a 2,270% increase in the cost of living since the creation of the Federal Reserve. So as one can see the debasement of the dollar's purchasing power on average per year is not too far removed from debasement of coinage in ancient Rome.

The founding fathers of the United States were learned and wise men. They knew full well the history of Roman money debasement, as well as the perils of paper money from their own personal history and experience. In the next two chapters we will examine the real world experiences the framers had with a paper money system run awry. From these experiences you will then understand why the framers were determined to write into law a sound money doctrine based on gold and silver as a foundation.

Gold and Silver: Money since Antiquity

Chapter 2

Paper Money Gains a Foothold

A Brief History

Money was rare in the early colonial days of America. Many of the earliest immigrants were very poor. They had few material resources to bring with them. What they found in America was bleak. Industry barely was developed. Goods and materials were in short supply. There were no banks. What money that circulated was thriftily consumed on supplies and basic life needs. Life was hard; and the absence of an abundant medium of exchange made life even harder.

Since the colonies were a developing economy a good sum of expenditure was spent on imports. This meant much of the gold and silver coin, or specie as it was called, was sent back abroad, usually to England.[1] Given that the export of specie from England to the colonies was barred by the English parliament a constant shortage of money prevailed in the colonies. Complicating the problem was that there were no mines in the colonies to dig for gold and silver for coinage. England furthermore banned the colonies from the right to mint coins. This led to an advanced form of barter for basic needs and necessities.[2]

---

[1] Specie is coined money. In our case specie will mean gold and silver.
[2] Corn, rice, wampum (sacred Indian shell beads) and fish were common items of barter.

Paper Money Gains a Foothold
Early American Growing Pains

There were many different types of barter arrangements in the colonies. Deer skins and beaver pelts were common mediums of exchange in rural areas where there were few settlers. So too was tobacco. In Virginia, Pennsylvania, Maryland, and the Carolinas tobacco was legal tender. Warehouse receipts circulated throughout the market place and were backed in full by tobacco in warehouses. Yet barter was a burdensome process that frustrated most parties, although it did not stop growth or westward expansion. Still, determining what to buy, sell and receive in a barter transaction without a universal equivalent or common medium was difficult in the extreme. Gold and silver coins were preferred. However, both were rare on the frontier.

With so many different mediums of exchange it was inevitable that the legislatures of the colonies would eventually attempt to standardize the monetary system. All did so according to their own fiercely independent needs. Massachusetts undertook one of the boldest measures. In defiance of the crown, the Massachusetts Bay Mint Act of May 27, 1652 was passed in an attempt to improve trade and commerce. The act established a mint for coinage of small denomination silver money, namely, shillings, three pence's, six pence's and twelve pence's.[3] A pine tree was the emblem on the coin. Basically, anybody could bring silver to the mint – spoons, forks, candlesticks, plates – and have them melted down into shillings and pence as prescribed in the law.[4] The mint lasted about thirty years. At that juncture the King of England, Charles II, ordered the mint closed[5] because it

---

[3] Shillings and pence (penny) were common English coins of the day.
[4] In practice the silver coins were minted with rather loose standards, and circulated at a sizeable discount.

encroached on the crown's rights and privileges. Nevertheless, such was the quantity of coins produced that they circulated in the colonies for over a century. Indeed, most agreed at the time that a crude silver coin was far better than wampum, deer skins and beaver pelts for every day commerce.

Given the rapid growth of the colonies and the need, yet inability, of merchants to obtain specie, less honorable methods were permitted. This took the form of privateering and buccaneering. The colonies knew their future lay in trade. Thus, during the great period of piracy between 1640 and 1680, a blind eye was turned toward pirates and buccaneers when their ships sailed into colonial ports. Large amounts of gold and silver coin were brought into the colonies, and as was their wont, the pirates and buccaneers spent their booty liberally, pouring precious specie into circulation.

The Spanish Milled Silver Dollar

Much of the pirate coinage originated from the Spanish West Indies where the Spanish silver dollar circulated widely.[6] The silver from these coins originated from mines in Bolivia, Peru and Mexico where the Spanish silver dollar was minted in vast quantities. Many of these coins found their way into the colonies as did gold coins from Portuguese Brazil. As it happened, the Spanish silver dollar became the leading coin of its day in America owing to its wide distribution, high standards and consistency of production,

---

[5] The mint apparently closed sometime around 1684 although the record is unclear on the actual date.
[6] The word dollar originated from a mispronunciation of the German word thaler, which was a silver coin that circulated in Europe from the year 1518.

Paper Money Gains a Foothold

which is to say it wasn't debased. An additional benefit was that the Spanish silver coin was subdivided into eight pieces, or *bits*, for ease of use and small denomination commerce.[7]

The adoption of the Spanish silver dollar had lasting impact. *Bits*, or eighths, were incorporated widely into popular language. When the stock exchanges eventually got up and running the term bit was immediately fused into the pricing vernacular. Up until the 1990's stocks traded in 1/8th increments, which is the system your author was trained on starting in 1983 as a stockbroker. Today stocks trade in one penny increments for the most part. But back in the day a stock quote was on the order of say, $9 ¾ by $9 7/8 rather than $9.49 by $9.50.

As the colonies grew in population, trade and wealth, a robust resistance against the English crown gained strength. Popular belief was that the crown was stifling growth by denying the colonies enough specie to meet the needs of a rapidly growing, dynamic economy demanding a common medium of exchange. To address the situation the colonies began to issue colonial currency, or paper money to be more precise.

The paper money issued by the American colonies was not the first time in the history of the world that a government had used paper money as a medium of exchange. It was the dynastic kingdoms of China that started the process of using paper money as a medium of exchange. Having created ink, paper and printing maybe it was

---

[7] A popular football cheer incorporated the term *bits*: *"2 bits, 4 bits, 6 bits, and a dollar etc. ..."*

inevitable that the Chinese developed the notion of paper money as well.[8]

The First Paper Money

The record is somewhat sketchy but starting sometime around the ninth century the first paper money appeared in China.[9] Over the next seven hundred years seven different Chinese dynasties used paper money. Every one of them had their own unique system. The end result in all cases was inflation of the money supply, and the eventual termination of the policy. Yet the people accepted paper money as their medium of exchange. Death awaited them if they didn't.

Sometime after the year 1500 the emission of paper money as governmental policy in China stopped although bank notes still circulated. As noted, the record is slim. But something dramatic must have happened. Hyperinflation and devaluation is known to have occurred. Once people and institutions become accustomed to a system of exchange a midcourse change of direction is difficult, especially after six or seven hundred years of the same policy. Based on the available evidence the Chinese reverted to a diverse arrangement of barter using a combination of silver coins, commodities and bank notes as mediums of exchange.[10]

---

[8] The Han dynasty used a white deerskin system of money in 206 BCE – 220 CE.
[9] There was a shortage of copper which was used to make coins during the reign of Hien Tsung from 806-821 CE.
[10] Gordon Tullock, Paper Money: A Cycle in Cathay. The Economic History Review, 1957.

War, Raids and a Failed Expedition

As students of American history know, the 1600's in the colonies were a time of constant warfare amongst the native Indians and the British, French, Dutch and Spanish colonialists. Massacres were all too common on both sides. Hitherto, the colonial conflicts were local affairs. At the same time, wars were being fought throughout the old world as well. Eventually, the old world wars and animosities were brought to the colonies. Fighting escalated when regular troops were brought into the colonies from France and England. All along the eastern seaboard during the 1600's the conflicts grew as the empires that had established colonies in America rubbed against each other. Thereupon it became common practice to form raiding parties with mixed forces of regular troops and colonists.

Almost always the purpose of a raid was revenge over one perceived infringement or the other. One of these occurred in 1690. It was then that a detachment of 1300 New Englanders and New Yorkers and a fleet of 35 British vessels set off for parts north in Canada in retaliation for a previous French raid in Schenectady, New York and some isolated settlements in New England. The target was Quebec City. The goal was revenge and booty. A victorious campaign would bring home heroes for the homefolk and enough booty to pay for the mission. Everybody would be happy. In this instance the French proved resilient, however, putting up a very effective resistance against the siege. Cold weather and small pox soon forced the combined British and colonial forces to retreat. This was on October 22, 1690.[11]

---

[11] This was the beginning of what came to be known as King William's War. It lasted for seven more years and set the stage for further British and French conflict in the colonies. It was the first of six wars fought in

Paper Money Gains a Foothold

Licking their wounds the colonial militiamen poured back into Boston in November 1690. Demoralized, and with no booty to sell for their efforts, the troops were a dispirited, starving, sickly lot to behold. Unfortunately, the Massachusetts Bay Colony was effectively insolvent at the time, and was counting on the booty to stimulate the economy and help meet ends. The colony also was in desperate need of a new charter from the King of England.

At the time all of the assets of the colony had reverted back to the King according to royal decree, including all of the land that the people were working. Thus, with no money to pay the troops for their efforts the Massachusetts Bay Colony faced a severe crisis what with a gang of starving, angry, mutinous men loitering around with nothing much to do. Out of generosity a few of the wealthier denizens of the colony gave the troops some specie. It wasn't near enough.

What to do? The options of the council leaders were few. The council dared not mint silver again and antagonize the King by violating the coinage privilege, it having been but a few years since Charles II angrily had closed the Massachusetts silver mint. Nor could the council leaders create a bank and make payments to the troops backed by land. A scant few years earlier just such a scheme had been tried and failed. And without a charter the land technically belonged to the King. So the council decided to print seven thousand pounds of paper money - or bills of credit as they called it – to pay the troops.

In reality the bills of credit were little more than IOU's. In order not to violate the King's privilege of legal tender

---

the colonies between Britain and France.

Paper Money Gains a Foothold

laws, the council didn't force the bills on the troops. The bills were offered only to the troops who wanted them. Upon accepting the bills the troops could use the bills to buy food, supplies, commodities and the like. Supposedly, the bills were backed by commodities such as corn, grain, cattle and silver. As a pre-condition the council promised to redeem the paper money in specie from collected tax revenue. However, the creditor class had to be appeased. This the council did by disallowing the paper money to be used to pay off private debts. There also was a promise not to issue any more paper after this one off event to pay the suffering troops.

So, in summation, whoever accepted the bills from the troops in exchange for selling his wares, could present the bills back to the Massachusetts Bay Colony as payment for taxes owed, or simply present the bills to the colony treasury and receive specie. The integrity and linchpin of the plan centered on the notion that the treasury when presented the bills actually would have specie on hand to pay the redeemer. This was in December 1690.

The pre-conditions soon were violated. A new charter, granted in 1691, gave the colony license to act with impunity. The leaders of the Massachusetts Bay Colony took full advantage of this window of opportunity. In one of the first acts under the new charter the full cost of the failed Quebec expedition was monetized by the council government. This amounted to forty thousand pounds. Paper money was printed and used to pay off the cost of the failed expedition.

Before long the public began to smell a rat. The paper money began to depreciate. Within the year the bills had depreciated by as much as forty percent against specie.

To alleviate the situation the council enacted more legislation. This time they made the paper money legal tender. The new paper could be used to pay off private debt at par as if it were specie. As a confidence booster, it was legislated that a five percent premium would be applied to the bills when used to pay taxes or debts owed to the council government. Again, the council promised that the new printing of forty thousand pounds would be the last of its kind.

Gresham's Law

The scheme did not work. Specie immediately disappeared from circulation providing a textbook example of Gresham's Law, which postulates that bad money drives out good money.[12] Rather than part with their precious silver and gold coins, given the legal tender status of paper money, the people simply exchanged the paper money for essentials in their day to day affairs.[13] Naturally, the prices of goods and services leaped in price. Nevertheless, other colonies took note of the happenings in Massachusetts, and made arrangements to do the same. They too began to issue paper money.

Much of the colonial paper money was denominated in pounds and shillings.[14] The problem was that specie disappeared from circulation almost precisely in correlation

---

[12] Gresham's law is named after Thomas Gresham, an Englishman who lived from 1519-1579. Before Gresham, both Copernicus and Aristophanes made note of this economic principle.

[13] "When a government compulsorily overvalues one type of money and undervalues another, the undervalued money will leave the country or disappear from circulation into hoards, while the overvalued money will flood into circulation." From Murray Rothbard, Commodity Money in Colonial America, page 47.

[14] Twenty shillings equaled one pound.

with the amount of new paper money created, exactly as Gresham's law said it would. So while the first emissions of paper money in the American colonies may have solved a short term problem, it created a more intractable, long term concern for the public. It drove specie out of circulation, and severely undermined the confidence in the monetary policies of the colonial assemblages.

Yet it was the colonial governments that benefited from the paper money. The governments were given license to print paper money and disgorge their debts at will. The people, on the other hand, suffered the ravages of inflation, depreciated money and higher prices. Little did the colonists know how long the new paper money system would persist as government policy. Until the revolution paper money would be one of the most common mediums of exchange throughout the colonies. This was not because the people liked paper money necessarily. The people were wise to the game. They simply held onto their Spanish silver dollars and such, and bought goods and services using legal tender paper money.

Ironically, the public was divided on hard money specie. For many, paper money was all they had ever known given that specie had gone underground. The thinking went like this. Specie was wealth to be held. Paper money was to be disgorged onto somebody else for real property.

In truth, some colonies managed their paper money better than others. Where there was good management, and limited printing, there was not too much stigma in paper money. Pennsylvania was an example of good stewardship. Fact was many merchants preferred paper money. The aristocracy was divided, too. Some were in favor of hard money; others weren't. Regardless of the divide, there wasn't enough specie in circulation to meet the satisfaction of a large percentage of the people owing to British restrictions and the iron law of Gresham. So the legislatures got creative.

In an effort to attract hard money and gain a competitive advantage, the colonies began to compete with each other to raise the lawful value of foreign coin such as the Spanish silver dollar. For example, a Spanish silver coin would be legally valued worth more than its equivalence in sterling. This ledger domain was accomplished through legislation passed by the various assemblies.

The crown Board of Trade in an effort to maintain some semblance of order drew up a proclamation creating a two tiered pricing level. According to the proclamation 100 pounds sterling in England was worth 133 pounds sterling in the colonies. Not to be outdone, the various colonies ratcheted the rate higher still. The rate was as high as 178 pounds sterling in some colonial areas.[15] Yet even these measures were insufficient to meet the demands of the fast developing colonial economy, and new waves of immigrants. It could be said that freedom and liberty has its advantages even amidst monetary chaos.

Paper money thus gained a foothold in colonial America more out of sheer opportunism rather than a free market resolution. English imperialism and intransigence prohibited wider use of specie in the colonies although it must be said that part of this stubbornness was due to a shortage of specie in England.

---

[15] E. James Ferguson, The Power of the Purse (Chapel Hill: The University of North Carolina Press, 1961) pp. 3-4.

Paper Money Gains a Foothold

In the main, British colonial policy centered on the notion that the colonies would provide raw material and revenue for the British Empire, and markets for British industry. Trade between the colonies and other nations was discouraged if not prohibited.[16] The quid pro quo would be British military protection. This thinking dovetailed with the notion that silver and gold specie ought not to be exported to the new world colonial backwater or *"plantations* "as Queen Anne referred to them.

For years the crown Board of Trade fought colonial attempts to institutionalize and inflate paper money. The colonists fought back just as hard. In reality it was a struggle over who would rule. One could even draw the conclusion that it was the debate over money that sowed the seeds of the revolution. But that's a discussion for another day.

Meanwhile, raids, reprisals, massacres, expeditions and imperial wars continued apace. To pay for these the colonial governments emitted larger and larger sums of paper money. Depreciation against specie was the inevitable result. By and large, specie remained underground except in those cases where merchants demanded specie over the alternative. The various colonial governments fought paper money depreciation tooth and nail. It was to no avail, however, despite threats of jail time, financial penalties and property seizures for failing to accept the paper money at par as legislated by law.

Exasperating the problem was that by forcing the people to accept depreciated paper money at par the governments themselves were forced to do the same insofar as accepting

---

[16] The Navigation Acts.

depreciated money from other colonies. For example, parked next door to Massachusetts was Rhode Island, whose money printing was legendary, and became a primary focus in the debate over a hard money standard at the Constitutional Convention of the States in 1787. But that was to come. In the meantime, paper money from Rhode Island poured into Massachusetts and depreciated the paper money of Massachusetts even more. Counterfeiting made the problem worse still.

The paper money schemes in the colonies essentially turned into a vicious cycle: the more paper money that was created the more specie was driven out of circulation. Few trusted the system; yet there was little alternative for the public except a cumbersome form of barter. By the middle of the 18th century so much money had been created in Massachusetts that the price of silver had soared tenfold from the jump date of 1690. Comparable depreciation levels were seen in the other colonies as well. In Rhode Island, however, the price of paper money sunk more than twenty to one versus specie. Prices of goods and services rose accordingly. The public was fed up. So was England.[17]

After the end of King George's War in 1748 England shipped to Massachusetts 650,000 ounces of Spanish silver dollars[18] and ten tons of copper as compensation for her war efforts.[19] The silver specie was used to retire the paper

---

[17] Queen Anne on June 18, 1704 decreed that the coin in the "plantations" be regulated according to their weight and fineness in proportion" to the Spanish milled silver dollar.
[18] Using silver specie as payment, The Massachusetts Currency Reform Act of 1749 called in the bills of credit for retirement. The 650,000 ounces of Spanish silver dollars represented 183, 649 pounds sterling. The silver was shipped in 217 chests from England.
[19] King George's War was another iteration of the French and Indian

Paper Money Gains a Foothold

money at a 7.5:1 paper to specie ratio. A second specie payment in 1750 of 310,000 ounces of Spanish silver dollars (87,435 pounds sterling) essentially put Massachusetts on a hard specie monetary system. After March 31, 1750 all contracts were expected to be settled in silver. The people of Massachusetts had until March 31, 1750 to turn in their paper money, after which it would be worthless. These actions ended the severe inflation in Massachusetts which had exceeded 19% each year between 1745 and 1749.

More changes were made. In 1751 England moved to institute new rules governing the printing of paper money in New England.[20] This was an effort to protect British industrialists and merchants once and for all from being paid in depreciated colonial paper money. Paper money printing still was allowed. But each print had to be backed by tax revenue sufficient to retire the emission within two years, five in the event of war. It was thought these measures would limit the depreciation of paper money if it came back into vogue.

A broader Act was passed in 1764. The 1764 Act enveloped all the British colonies in America, and prohibited the use of paper money as legal tender for public and private debts. The same act required the colonies to retire their paper money as it returned to the treasury in the form of tax

---

wars fought primarily in Massachusetts, New York, New Hampshire and Nova Scotia. This war was fought between 1744 and 1748. Some eight percent of the adult male population of Massachusetts was killed in the fighting.

[20] New England was defined as the colonies or plantations of Rhode Island, the Providence plantations, Connecticut, Massachusetts and New Hampshire. Paper money in New England was not allowed to be legal tender under the Parliament legislation.

revenue. Interestingly, the 1764 Act did not disallow the printing of paper money.

The French and Indian War ended in 1763. It had broken out in 1754 between Britain and France over markets, territory, and land and over who ultimately would rule America. The fighting was over a large expanse in the colonies from Virginia to Nova Scotia. Eventually, the British won the war with tremendous support from the colonies in both life and treasure.

At the end of the war the colonies emerged in decent financial shape. The British had spent huge sums in the colonies during the war, and had subsidized the colonial governments heavily. Thus, Britain exited the war with a national debt that had doubled. In point of fact, the British would soon move to reduce that debt by taxing the colonies which would sow the seeds for the revolution. But that was down the road.

As soon as the French and Indian War ended the colonies began to reduce their debt obligations. The colonies also began a vigorous campaign to reverse the Currency Act of 1764 after its passage. With the progress of time those who knew life before paper money was the norm were few and far between.

One of the chief proponents of the paper money system as it turns out was Benjamin Franklin. Maybe this was because as a Pennsylvanian he had not lived under the more disastrous effects of paper money depreciation as had the people of Massachusetts, Rhode Island and North Carolina. Nevertheless, Franklin lobbied the crown to repeal the restrictive Currency Act.

Paper Money Gains a Foothold

Franklin's goal was to form land banks funded by British money. The project stalled, however, when it became apparent that British approval of the plan centered on the crown's desire to appropriate the revenue streams originating from land bank deals. The project thus took a back seat. In its stead a new issue took stage front and center, and that was the tax issue. As everyone knows it would lead to war and revolution.[21]

Summary

Paper money once established as legal tender eventually is printed until it is devalued and rejected by the market.

Paper money relies on the virtue and discipline of the men printing and issuing the currency. Man is fallible. Eventually a generation of men will arise that are willing to print the people's way to prosperity. From then on it is a matter of time until the paper money is printed in such quantity that it is devalued and rejected by the free market.

The much repeated course of paper money schemes usually transpire in the following mannerism. The paper money is first issued. Hard money disappears as per Gresham's Law. The paper is counterfeited. New paper money is created to replace the counterfeited paper. Massive printing of the paper takes place. Depreciation of the paper takes hold. Eventually the paper money is rejected by the free market.

<u>Paper Money. Unlimited Printing. Eventually Rejected</u>

---

[21] Ferguson, The Power of the Purse, 23.

Chapter 3

The Continental: Hell's Half Acre

War, Inflation and Paper Money

The tax and political issues leading to the American Revolution are well known. Most students of American history are familiar with the Sugar Act, the Stamp Act, the Quartering Act, the Tea Act, and the Intolerable Acts and so on and so forth. Suffice to say, rebellion, war and revolution broke out between the American colonies and England in June 1775. When hostilities opened, new conventions, legislatures and constitutions were in the process of replacing the royalist charters of the day. Events demanded an army which soon formed.

At the time there was no central government or treasury. Congress had to shoulder the role of both. First and foremost in the mind of Congress was determining a way to pay for the war. There were three ways: tax, borrow or print. It was clear a general tax to pay for the war was out of the question given the visceral public reaction to British tax hikes. Loans and aid from foreign countries were not yet forthcoming. Paper money and printing was the path of least resistance. As the revolution intensified the printing of paper money, or fiat currency, took off like a rocket.[1] At the same time, gold and silver all but disappeared from circulation as

---

[1] Fiat money derives its value from government regulation or law. The term fiat originates from Latin meaning "let it be done" or "it shall be." Where it exists fiat money circulates by government decree.

people gripped ever tighter their sole means of defense against debasement and devaluation. Practically speaking, paper money was printed and handed over to government officials, officers, quartermasters and the like for the purchase of arms, supplies, food and wages for the troops. The paper money was called the Continental. Those colonists loyal to the crown would have nothing to do with the Continental. They refused to accept it in areas under firm British control, or rid themselves of it as soon as humanly possible when it was forced on them. Patriotic Americans, however, accepted the Continental.

Needless to say, war is an expensive enterprise, especially long wars. And given that the colonies could increase the money supply only by printing ever more Continentals the resulting depreciation was inevitable. This was proven to be true. The longer the war lasted the greater the depreciation became.

Yet there was hope in the beginning. Rules were established. One of these was that each state was charged with retiring the Continental in the out years starting in 1779 on a pro-rata basis per state based on population.

In the early stages of the war the Continental was not legal tender. It was produced in small denominations for use in day to day transactions as a common medium of exchange, and for payment of taxes.

The Continental

The first float of the Continental was a two million dollar print in June 1775. A one million dollar print came close on its heels in July. Before the year was out a full six million in Continentals had been printed.[2] To give perspective to these six million dollars, keep in mind the original monetary base in the colonies in July 1775 was estimated at twelve million dollars. Therefore, in but a short seven months, the money supply had exploded by 50%, or an annualized rate of almost 100%. At the same time some of the colonies started issuing their own brand of paper money separate from that of the Continental. In retrospect, it is easy to see where all of this was leading.

Initially, the circulation of the Continental had a positive effect on the people. Farm and agricultural prices increased much to the pleasure of farmers. Because of the firming of prices many would-be farmers rushed into the breach and bought farms anticipating the boom to continue. Little did they note that input costs were rising side by side with the increase in agricultural prices. But as input prices continued spiking along with the cost of finished goods at market the grumbling began.

At the beginning of 1776 the Continental basically had held its value given what might be expected in wartime. But in January of that year the purchasing power of the Continental began to cave. As people began to sense the coming disaster, they started to discount the Continental. On January 11, 1776 Congress found it necessary to issue a preamble deeming those refusing to accept the Continental at par as an *"enemy of his country."* This was just the beginning of the heavy handed tactics to be implemented by the authorities to force the people to accept the Continental at par.

---

[2] Ferguson, The Power of the Purse, p. 26.

The Continental: Hell's Half Acre

On February 17, 1776 the treasury was established. A team of five was selected. The team soon had plenty to do. In the blinking of an eye the revolution swallowed the first six million dollar print of the Continental. Thus, a nineteen million dollars fiat suit was authorized and printed in 1776. In 1777 thirteen million Continentals were printed; in 1778 sixty four million dollars were printed, only to be followed by a whopping one hundred and forty million dollar print in 1779.

In all, some $242 million dollars of paper money were printed in a short five year period. This barrage of paper overwhelmed the original twelve million dollar money supply that existed in the colonies at the start of the revolution. All in all the money supply expanded in five short years by roughly 1,916%.

The amount of paper printed was too much for the economy to absorb. The first signs of destruction appeared in the autumn of 1776. Prices started to rise, and support of the Continental by patriotic Americans began to wane. In the marketplace the Continental began to drop as well. At the end of 1775 the Continental maintained about 90% of its original value. By the end of 1776 it had lost one-third of its value. The drop then picked up speed in 1777 when it lost two-thirds of its value. And on and on it went until by 1780 the Continental basically was worthless. Large scale British counterfeiting hurt confidence in the Continental as well. But the amount of paper money printed simply overwhelmed the economy. Observed a different way, at the beginning of the war one could buy $1 in silver specie with $1.25 in Continental paper. By April of 1781 it took $168 paper Continentals to buy $1 in silver specie.

The Continental: Hell's Half Acre

On top of the Continental disaster, a few states as noted issued their own forms of paper money. By 1783 the sum of $210 million had been issued. This exercise ended in disaster as well, and for the same reason as the demise of the Continental. Too many were issued; they depreciated and eventually became worthless.

The Human Effects of the Continental

The power of the currency debacle had a severe effect on the people. In late September 1776, the quartermaster of New Jersey reported that his representatives could not buy grain using the Continental. The sellers demanded gold or silver. A shoemaker was declared an enemy of the state because he refused the Continental. In another instance a hospital refused payment in Continentals. These are not isolated examples. The number of instances rose congruently with the drop in value of the Continental. Penalties were imposed on those who refused to accept the Continental. Usually this took the form of seizing the property of the poor 'guilty' soul who refused acceptance. In other cases the business establishment of the 'guilty' person was closed. This latter attempt at retribution stopped, however, when the competitors of the accused raised their prices in lieu of their new-found monopoly pricing power.

To force acceptance of the Continental severe measures were undertaken.[3] The Continental was made legal tender. Wage and price controls were implemented. Restrictions were placed on the amount of markup a retailer

---

[3] Congress passed a resolution stating that *"whoever should refuse to receive in payment Continental bills, should be declared and treated as an enemy of his country and be excluded from inter-course with its inhabitants"*.

could charge for imported products. In this case merchants simply quit importing. Additionally, laws were enacted prohibiting the withholding of key military items. People were forbidden from stocking up on goods above and beyond what was deemed necessary for their family. Retailers were prohibited from overcharging as well. Snitches were on the lookout, too. Overcharging for the established price of an item subjected the accused to public humiliation, but usually the party was released upon agreeing to live by the rules and snitch on others. Even bartering was labeled a suspicious activity.

Initially, George Washington was aghast at the lack of patriotism of the people. He saw no reason not to accept the Continental. In September 1777, Washington wrote that while he would happily accept the Continental as payment for rents of his property he expected to get payment in the amount relative to the value of his property. Later, in 1778, Washington wrote that he would only trade land for land in a deal that he was transacting during the war, lest he lose money if he accepted the Continental. Yet it was Washington who had written earlier in the war of hanging *"monopolizers, forestallers, and engrossers."*[4]

"It is much to be lamented", Washington wrote, they had not been hunted down like the "pests" they were, and hung in the public square. By August 1779, however, Washington had seen the light and come full circle, refusing to accept the Continental for rents agreed upon before the revolution unless other citizens did likewise. Indeed, Washington said in April 1779, *"A wagon load of money will*

---

[4] *Forestallers* and *engrossers* bought most or all of an essential supply, and then marked up the price drastically: same thing for *monopolizers*.

scarcely purchase a wagon load of provisions". To his credit Washington to his dying day became an adamant foe of paper money; and he did everything in his power to never allow the malicious effects of paper money to gain another foothold in America after the revolution. A decade after the war he was just as adamant. Writing in 1787, Washington said that *"paper money ... [will] ... ruin commerce, oppress the honest, and open the door to every species of fraud and injustice."*[5]

As noted earlier, the people were equally aggrieved with the debasement of the Continental. The longer the war dragged on the worse the situation got. At the point of bayonet army quartermasters began to confiscate provisions and resources from merchants and traders who were accused of withholding essential supplies. As prices increased under the relentless issuance of paper the people turned on each other. City dwellers accused country folk of withholding food and grain. Those living in the country accused city dwellers of blackmail and coercion. Pamphlets were produced and distributed accusing merchants and tradesmen of price gouging. Death was threatened on the accused. Unfortunately, these were not isolated pockets of discontent. They were patterns of behavior and desperation both wide and deep throughout the land. In normal times most people never would have behaved in such fashion. But the catalyst of money printing, war and revolution pushed normally happy people to the edge of their ability to cope.

---

[5] Horace White, Money and Banking (Boston: Ginn and Co., 1902) Chapter II: Revolutionary Bills of Credit, pp. 115-130.

Hyperinflation, Death and Disease

On top of these trepidations, small pox broke out. Beginning in 1775, the pox spread over most of the eastern seaboard from Canada to Florida and into the Great Plains, over to New Mexico and eventually up to present day Washington State, and even Alaska. It is estimated that some 145,000 people were killed in the small pox epidemic, which ended sometime in 1782. To add perspective roughly 7200 American soldiers were killed in battle during the revolution. Maybe 10,000 died of various diseases and exposure, while about 8-9000 died in British prison camps. The sum of the revolutionary dead totals roughly 25,000. Thus, the dead from the pox was roughly six times the dead from the war.

Soldiers serving in the American army were inoculated against the pox, but they suffered no less. As the war wore on, some threatened mutiny. Others fought starvation and all but died from poor health, diet and exposure. Their pay, of course, was all but non-existent as the Continental plummeted. It was a dog eat dog world of pain, disease, suffering and struggle for survival. Reading the historical accounts of the day it's a testament to the toughness of the American people that the war was carried through to the end. Some commentators have noted that had the people known what was in store for them to rid themselves of the British it's questionable whether they would have chosen to revolt.

The Continental is Retired

In the meantime, the Congress and people had had enough of paper money. By Act of Congress on July 28, 1780, the Continental was authorized for redemption at the prevailing market rate in Spanish milled silver dollars. The exchange rate was about 2.5% of the face amount. On May 31, 1781 the Continental stopped circulating as money through another Act of Congress.

Silver specie used to retire the Continental came from France, which offered her services to help the colonies defeat the British. Also of historical interest, a tidy sum of specie came from the British, whose troops and government spent significant sums in the colonies for supplies and the like. Indeed, from 1780 until the end of the war specie was in plentiful supply much to the relief of all.

Summary

The war contributed, but the printing of the Continental, led to many unintended consequences. A fair portion of the population was destroyed not only by disease and war, but also by the crazy hyperinflation of the currency. Few escaped the maelstrom. Fortunes were lost. Families and neighbors turned against each other. People starved. Few people knew who to trust. Eventually, the Continental, as all paper money systems, collapsed and was rejected.

Once hard money started circulating again in the colonies at the end of the war a deflation of assets began to assert itself. This was inevitable after the huge inflation of the Continental. Among the many groups that suffered under falling prices were farmers, particularly the ones mentioned at the beginning of the chapter. These were the men who rushed into the breach at the beginning of the war, buying farms as agricultural prices increased. Now they saw the opposite effect as both agricultural prices and the value of their property fell in lockstep as sound money overtook paper money at the end of the war.

The framers of the Constitution took note of all these developments, and resolved – never again. The notes James Madison wrote down at the Constitutional Convention in 1787, and meticulously re-drafted at the end of each day, prove this conclusively. While it is true that paper money might have been the only way to "*pay*" for the revolution and freedom, it's equally true that the piper will be paid at the point when the war ends and the paper scheme is unwound. This was true with the Continental, the Greenback, the Confederate dollar, the Papiermark after World War I and the Reichsmark after World War II. Paper money is a failed monetary policy. It doesn't work.

One might make an agreement with the devil; but in the end the devil will meet you in hell.

The Continental. Lesson Learned. Never Again

Chapter 4

The Constitutional Dollar: 1792-2012

Bimetallism

Bimetallism is a monetary standard where the value of the monetary unit is defined as equivalent both to a certain quantity of gold and to a certain quantity of silver. Bimetallism establishes a fixed rate of exchange between gold and silver.

Once the revolution ended the new American government set about establishing new customs for its money. The first Secretary of the Treasury, Alexander Hamilton, meticulously studied the virtues of a gold based versus a silver based currency. He proposed both, recommending a dual metallic system similar to the one practiced by England.[1]

To properly understand the motivation why the framers took the steps they did one has to understand the context of the times. Reading the Constitution is not enough. Language and linguistic differences abound for the modern reader. Although it would be enjoyable to discuss more about the context of the times what is germane to our discussion is that the debacle of paper money still was fresh in public consciousness. Interestingly, many of the Constitutional Convention delegates were the very ones who

---

[1] From 1605 until 1816 England was on a bimetallic standard. In 1816 England adopted the gold standard.

had promulgated the disaster that was the Continental. Now these same delegates had repaired to Philadelphia to take up one of the very issues that had caused so much pain and suffering. In this instance, rather than defending their disastrous policies, the delegates made a U-turn.

Transcripts of the debates in the Constitutional Convention of the States in 1787 bear this out. The first drafts of the Constitution included language allowing the federal government to issue paper money. This was due to the fact that early drafts of the Constitution used the Articles of Confederation written in 1777 as a foundation, not because the framers had any intention of allowing paper money. Once the topic of money came up for debate the proposal met stiff resistance. Edmund Randolph made this point clear when he asserted that, while the Articles of Confederation allowed paper money, it only did so because *"the havoc of paper money had not been foreseen."*[2]

Little doubt existed that the framers intended to establish a hard money system of commerce. This applied to the states as well. James Madison noted that a major reason for the Convention was to address *"the internal administration of the States"* wherein *"violation(s) of contracts had become familiar, in the form of depreciated paper made a legal tender."*[3] Another delegate, Roger Sherman, the author of Article 1, Section 10 of the Constitution, favored a total prohibition against states issuing their own paper money.

---

[2] E. H. Scott, Journal of the Federal Convention (Chicago: Albert, Scott & Co., 1894), page 60, Cornell University Library.
http://www.archive.org/details/cu31924009891684
[3] Scott, Journal of the Federal Convention, page 47.

The Constitutional Dollar: 1792-2012

On August 16, 1787 the Convention delegates took up a measure to disallow the government the right to print paper money.[4] The vote was overwhelming against paper money. Clearly the attitude of the framers toward paper money was that of derision and disapproval. Having experienced firsthand the risks of paper money the framers banned the national government from instituting the practice and the states from possessing the power to *"emit bills* (paper money) *of credit, nor make anything but gold and silver coin a tender in payment of debts"*.

Studying the Constitution one finds twice the mention of the word *dollar*. Yet the word *dollar* is not defined. The reason for this is that at the time the Constitution was drafted everyone knew that money was largely identical to a weight and measure of silver and gold coins, and the *dollar* was equivalent in meaning to the Spanish silver milled dollar. But the Constitution did not define the weight or measure of the *dollar*. The final decision on the exact weight and measure for the *dollar* was left to Congress.

Congress responded by passing the Coinage Act on April 2, 1792. In this legislation the silver dollar was established as the unit of money in the United States. The Coinage Act valued gold in weight against silver, and vice-versa.

The result was that by law both silver and gold were connected to each other with equal standing in law.[5] In

---

[4] Edward J. Larson and Michael P. Winship, The Constitutional Convention (New York: The Modern Library Paperback Edition, 2005), p. 124.
[5] Murray N. Rothbard, A History of Money and Banking in the United States: The colonial Era to World War II (Auburn, Alabama: Ludwig

addition, legal tender status was accorded silver and gold. The Coinage Act also produced a decimal system for United States currency. A prior act established the copper penny.

The Weight and Measure of a *Dollar*

The Coinage Act of 1792 established the weight and measure for silver money in dollars or units. The *dollar* was defined as 371 4/16 grains pure silver. This is what is meant when you hear the term "constitutional money." By definition a constitutional dollar is 371 4/16 grains pure silver.

Gold was to be minted as well. The Coinage Act defined gold in relation to silver on a 15 to 1 ratio. The gold coins were to be called eagles.[6] A $10 gold eagle was set at 247 4/8 grains pure gold, a $5 half eagle at 123 6/8 grains pure gold and a $2.50 quarter eagles at 61 7/8 grains pure gold. Thus, $10 dollars equaled 3712.5 grains pure silver, or 247.5 grains pure gold.[7]

Free Coinage

The *dollar*, as noted, was defined in law as a fixed weight and measure of silver and gold. But where did the coins come from, and who issued them? In actual fact, it was the role of the people – the free market – to bring their own gold and silver to the mint, and coin their own money. The government's role was to melt down the gold and silver and

---

Von Mises Institute, 2002) page 66.
[6] A $10 eagle was set "to be of the value of ten dollars or units." This meant that a $10 gold eagle originated by weight and measurement from a silver dollar or unit. A $1 gold coin didn't appear until 1849.
[7] Rozeff, Michael S., The U.S. Constitution and Money: Corruption and Decline. The Writer's Free Internet Edition – Volume III. (East Amherst, 2010) Chapter 1.

put the government's seal, or stamp of approval, on the coin at the specified weight and measure per coin. This is what is meant by free coinage of silver and gold, and it is the monetary system the framers created for the United States. It was the people – the free market – that were in charge of the actual money supply and money creation. The government simply maintained the standards of the coins based on the prescribed weight and measures laid out in the Coinage Act.

Supply and Demand

As the framers knew all too well the problem with bimetallism – using both silver and gold coins at the same time for commerce - is that once the ratio is fixed it doesn't stay static in the free market. Each metal moves in price according to its own dynamics. This is exactly what happened with silver almost immediately after the framers set the ratio at 15:1 versus gold in the Coinage Act.[8] The price of silver began to depreciate versus gold. With the advent of the hard money medium of exchange, hoarded and buried silver specie immediately began to circulate in the new American states. In addition, worldwide mining, production and importation of silver climbed as time went by resulting in an excess of supply which naturally led to a drop in the free market price of silver.[9]

The ratio of silver to gold dropped from 15:1 to 15.75:1. The result was that gold coins dropped out of circulation with silver coins remaining the principle means of exchange in the economy. This is a textbook example of

---

[8] The ratio had fluctuated for a few thousand years between 10-15:1.
[9] Laughlin, J. Laurence, The History of Bimetallism in the United States (New York: D. Appleton and Co., 1898) Chapter 1, The Arguments of Bimetallists and Monometallists.

Gresham's Law, which contends that in a dual monetary system where two or more metals have legal tender status, the cheaper metal money will drive out of circulation the more expensive metal money in payment for goods and services. In this case that's exactly what happened. People wanted to hold on to their higher valued gold coins and use silver coins as a means of exchange given that both were legal tender, and the exchange rate was set by law.[10]

Because of the dropping silver to gold ratio the United States essentially was on a silver standard from 1792-1834. Indeed, silver was the principle medium of exchange throughout this period. However, in 1834 the Jackson administration devalued gold. This ended the long de facto silver standard period in the United States, and brought on what amounted to a de facto gold standard even though nothing had changed constitutionally. Upon the Jackson administration's actions the ratio of silver to gold was set at 16:1. Gold was priced at $20.67.

Subsequent to the discovery of gold in California in 1848, as well as discoveries in Russia and Australia, the price of gold dropped further owing to the laws of supply and demand. It was the same situation that had existed after the passage of the 1792 Coinage Act, except this time it was gold, not silver, that was used primarily as a means of exchange. And with the silver to gold ratio dropping, Gresham's Law once again came into play. Silver basically

---

[10] A modern day example of this phenomenon is the ninety percent 1964 Kennedy silver half-dollars. As the price of silver increased the ninety percent silver content Kennedy halves (and forty percent) all but ceased to circulate as hoarders and collectors held onto them for their silver content, while the post 1964/5 halves with no silver content remained in circulation. The same situation occurred with dimes, quarters and so on and so forth.

fell out of favor, the result being that the United States was on a gold standard in all but name and law until 1933, not counting the periods of war.

Bimetallism: 1792-1873

The silver and gold bimetallic standard functioned fairly well in the 19th century with the notable exceptions of the War of 1812 and the Civil War. Just as one might expect the same issues emerged in 1812 and 1861 as had existed in 1775, namely, how to pay for the wars: tax, borrow, print or some combination of the three?

In the War of 1812 banks were allowed to suspend specie payments. After a sizeable expansion of loans and credit preceding the war many of the banks in the United States faced bankruptcy when conditions took a turn for the worse. This left the people once again under the Sheol of paper money as had been the case during the revolution thirty years earlier.

Essentially what happened was that banks outside the New England area made a vast amount of loans.[11] Many of the bank notes (paper money) created in these transactions wound up in New England where munitions factories existed. Eventually these bank notes were deposited in New England banks. Around 1814 the New England banks began to demand the issuing banks - primarily located in the South, West and Mid-Atlantic states – to exchange the notes as contractually obligated for specie. With not enough specie to

---

[11] After the first national bank of the United States was closed, the government placed all their deposits in state banks around the country. With these new deposits the state banks vastly expanded their loan portfolios.

meet redemptions of the notes these banks faced immediate bankruptcy.

In the face of this disaster, the government allowed the suspension of specie, which is to say, the banks did not have to exchange their paper money for gold and silver as they had promised to users of their paper money. Yet these defaulting banks were allowed to continue as going concerns. At the same time, the banks expected their outstanding loans to be paid even as these same banks had broken their own contractual rights.

Specie redemptions resumed after two and on-half years. But precedence had been established. From 1814 until after the Civil War, troubled banks were allowed to suspend specie payments each time an inflation and credit binge was met with demands for redemptions in gold and silver. Examples are the panics of 1819, 1837, 1839 and 1861. For all intents and purposes it was obvious a pattern had emerged. Each time a crisis erupted the bankers demanded and were allowed to evade their contractual obligations even as the result of a self-inflicted wound.

On December 30, 1861 the banks suspended specie payments after the outbreak of the Civil War. Close on the heels of this decision was one by the Treasury to also suspended specie redemptions on its treasury notes.[12] The next step, of course, was the creation of paper money which became known as greenbacks. These latter were created in February 1862, and made legal tender for all debts. $150 million in greenbacks immediately were printed to pay for

---

[12] Interest payments on treasury notes remained payable in specie.

the war effort. Eventually $450 million greenbacks were authorized.

Predictable results ensued. Gold and silver were driven out of circulation, and the greenbacks began to trade at a considerable discount. The Secretary of the Treasury Salmon Chase made every effort to stop the decline. Enacting taxes and duties on gold, he restricted bank loans using gold as collateral above its face value, and he intervened in the market by selling treasury gold in an attempt to manipulate the price downward. Chase failed at every turn. But he didn't give up the attempt to defeat the free market.

A scheme was hatched to curtail the devaluation of the greenback by aggressively intervening in the foreign exchange market. It failed. In a final desperate maneuver he rammed through Congress legislation entitled "An Act to Prohibit Certain Sales of Gold and Foreign Exchange" which outlawed the trading of foreign currency longer than ten days into the future. The legislation also banned futures trading of gold as well with a stipulation that all gold sales be enacted only through his department. Amid chaos in the gold market the legislative effort failed. The greenback dropped abruptly twenty percent and the legislation was repealed two weeks later. The damage was done however. It had started the instant that paper money was reintroduced in 1862. And it would not end until the war was over and cooler heads prevailed.

The United States was still on a paper money standard in 1873 when Congress made changes to the mint and coinage regulations. There were few coins of silver denomination in circulation in 1873 owing to the discovery of gold in California in 1848, which caught the attention of world. With vast new quantities of gold hitting the market the price of gold dropped in relation to silver. The flip side to this was that silver was worth more in terms of gold than it had been previously. As the premium in silver ratcheted upward, silver coins were pulled from circulation vis-a-vis Gresham's Law. There's more to the story but the long and short of it is that a lot of silver was exported east, particularly to India.[13] Therefore, by the time Congress made the decision to change the mint and coinage laws the people were more familiar with gold than silver. Thus, there was little push back when Congress discontinued the free coinage of silver, at least initially. The net effect of the Coinage Act of 1873 was that it ended the bimetallic monetary system that had existed since the Coinage Act of 1792.

The Advent of the Gold Standard

In 1873 the United States was still on a paper money system stemming from the Civil War. That changed on January 1, 1879 when the United States returned to hard money. This was the date established upon passage of another Act of Congress called the Specie Resumption Act of 1875 stipulating that greenbacks would be redeemed at par in specie. Technically, the country was placed on a gold standard although the law didn't explicitly say so. Once the Specie Resumption Act of 1875 was passed critics of the new policy became very vocal in opposition to the fact that gold - and only gold - would be bestowed free coinage at the mint. A war of words would flare up from time to time over

---

[13] India started importing silver from the United States rather than Russia due to the Crimean War. A second reason was that Indian cotton producers gained at the expense of her American counterparts during the American Civil War, giving India greater income to import silver.

the next two decades over what critics and detractors called the "crime of 1873."[14]

The technical issue of the gold standard in the United States finally was resolved in 1900 when the Gold Standard Act was passed. The Act fixed the dollar at 25.8 grains gold given ninety percent purity. A price of $20.67 per ounce was established, exactly as it had been priced 66 years earlier under the Jackson administration.

The period from 1879 to 1914 has been labeled by many commentators as the premier age of the gold standard. Most major countries adhered in varying degrees to the gold standard. The period was relatively calm in terms of geopolitical gamesmanship and war, thus allowing for strong economic growth and international trade.[15] Peace and prosperity, however, broke down with the start of World War I. Within weeks of the outbreak of hostilities in August 1914 the major European powers were scuttling the gold standard, and instituting a paper money system. Among the major world powers the United States was the one country that did not exit the gold standard in World War I, although the United States did cease to export gold until after the end of the war.

---

[14] The Bland-Allison Act passed in 1878 stipulated that the government buy anywhere from two to four million dollars per month in silver for small denomination coinage. This Act was designed to appease a broad but loosely organized group that opposed the mono-metallic gold standard.

[15] The wars of the period count the 1894/5 war between Japan and China, the 1895/8 Spanish-American War and the Anglo-Boer conflict fought in South Africa in 1900.

The Constitutional Dollar: 1792-2012

The Gold Exchange Standard

A short while after the end of World War I in 1926 the gold exchange standard was initiated. The gold exchange standard was a fixed exchange rate system whereby the United States pegged the dollar to gold while other countries pegged their currencies to the dollar. In short, the United States stayed on the traditional gold standard, agreeing to exchange dollars for gold on demand. At the same time, other countries around the world returned to a quasi-gold standard. For example, British pounds or Dutch guilders and other currencies were redeemable in gold bars but not gold coins. In practice this made the exchange mechanism suitable for large scale international dealings at the expense of the man in the street that had as ever to grin and bear the burden of paper money inflation. So the gold exchange standard was not a true gold standard in the real meaning of the definition, although Americans still could exchange their dollars for gold at $20.67 per ounce.

The British pound was a key part of the gold exchange system. At the Genoa Conference in 1922 the pound was made exchangeable into gold bullion bars for international customers. Yet the pound was the weak link in the gold exchange system. The problem lay in the fact that Britain moved back onto the pre-World War I level of the pound at $4.86 not accounting for the huge inflation of the money supply and debt to pay for the war. The decision to peg the pound to the dollar at $4.86 was made more out of national pride than any monetary factor. The pound thus was valued too highly to account for Britain's rapidly increasing welfare state and all the money printed during the World War I.

Yet the British had willing accomplices in the gold exchange scheme. The British were able to cajole their trade partners into inflating their own money supply in lock step with her. Therefore there was not a self-enforcing mechanism in the gold exchange system to force the British government to defray from printing money and inflating the money supply. Nor did the British want a constraining mechanism. The goal was to promote exports and revive the peace-time economy. Yet that's precisely what every other country wanted to do for itself as well.

Enabling the British in the gold exchange scheme was the United States Federal Reserve which ran a pro-British monetary policy through its own money printing and inflationary policy. This policy by the Fed essentially provided cover for the British to inflate and run budget deficits without fear of losing their dollar reserves or gold to the United States. So the gold exchange system was not really a gold standard at all. It was a ruse which saw the United States enabling an inflationary policy by the British who cavorted with her trade partners to also run an inflationary policy. It was more of a giant inflationary Ponzi scheme than sound monetary policy where everybody was in on the game except the man in the street that paid for it unwittingly in higher prices. The long and short of the gold exchange system is that it lasted from 1926 until 1931 when it collapsed from its own flaws.

Bretton Woods

In Chapter 6 I'll discuss in detail the decision by the Roosevelt administration to exit the gold standard in 1933. So at this point I'll skip that lengthy and important moment in history. In the meantime, let's discuss the next step in the evolution of the monetary system in the United States. This development arose from a meeting in Bretton Woods, New Hampshire. Out of this meeting came what is called the Bretton Woods Agreement. The year was 1944. At the conference were 730 delegates representing 44 nations. As the reader well knows World War II was still raging at the time. Yet the Allied powers sensed an Allied victory, and moved forward on monetary plans for the post-war period.

The thrust of the Bretton Woods Agreement was the establishment of a set of rules, institutions and practices to regulate the international monetary system post-war. The United States dollar was recognized as the *"reserve"* currency against which other countries would peg their currency. Each currency was allowed to trade and fluctuate within a narrow band of one percent against the dollar. To maintain the trading band, institutions were formed to oversee and implement the targets. These were the International Monetary Fund and the International Bank for Reconstruction and Development. Basically, member countries were charged with buying and selling dollars in the foreign exchange market to maintain their peg within the one percent band against the dollar.

For its part, the United States agreed to peg the dollar against gold at $35 per ounce. Yet $35 per ounce of gold represented the pre-World War II price of gold, and failed to account for the enormous increase in spending and debt that the United States had undertaken during World War II. Of course, the debt and deficits in the United States resulting from the war effort are relative insofar as they are compared to the utter devastation of the infrastructures and economy's' of many of the signers of the Bretton Woods Agreement.

The Constitutional Dollar: 1792-2012

That said, in 1944 the United States owned some sixty percent of the world's gold reserves. So there was wiggle room for the United States for fixing the dollar to gold at such a low level. The dollar thus was made to play the role that gold had played under the gold standard. Indeed, the United States agreed to exchange dollars for gold for those countries that preferred gold. As for the other signatories, their currencies traded relative to the dollar, not gold. The dollar was the one currency fixed against gold.

The Bretton Woods agreement lasted until 1971. At that point the United States completely abandoned the dollar link to gold. In essence the dollar in 1971 became the Continental.

This brings us to where we are today. Since 1971 the United States has been on a paper money currency system. Sound money has been at the mercy of Federal Reserve chairmen. The results have been far from satisfactory. National debt, trade deficits and fiscal deficits have continued to increase as ever more and larger amounts of paper money have been printed as in the revolutionary days of the Continental. Indeed, since 1971 when the United States severed all ties of redemption between the dollar and gold, the dollar has lost over 80% of its purchasing power. In addition, the value of the dollar as everyone knows has plummeted to some $1/1900^{th}$ to the ounce as gold has risen north of $1900 per ounce.

Competitive devaluations to promote exports and currency wars have been the main feature of life after the breaking of the gold tie. In the midst of the long term devaluation of the dollar, holders of gold and silver have maintained their purchasing power even though it has been a

The Constitutional Dollar: 1792-2012

wild ride. As has been said - an ounce of gold is still an ounce of gold. That can't be said for the dollar.

The Gold Standard Explained

There are several different types of gold standards that have existed through the ages. For a significant part of her history the United States operated under a bimetallic silver and gold standard. The problem with bimetallism is that the fixed ratio between the two metals is constantly being challenged. This leads to periodic episodes where one or the other metals disappears from circulation according to Gresham's Law, as prudent holders cling to the more expensive metal, and spend the less costly one. This happened in the old Roman Empire. It happened in the United States as well.

From 1879 until 1933 the gold coin standard was operational in the United States. The key characteristics of the gold coin standard are these. Paper money is held on an equal footing with a gold coined unit. The paper money is defined by an equal and equivalent amount of gold and can be exchanged for gold, or converted into gold if you will, on request.

As for gold, the public is at liberty to coin it at the mint without egregious charges or obstruction. Free flow of gold coins in the economy is a mainstay of the gold coin standard. The public can do as they please with gold coins. They can be melted down and recast as candlesticks, rings, necklaces or whatever the owner desires. The gold coins can be exported or imported with impunity. A final feature of the gold coin standard is that gold coin needs be a significant share of the country's monetary reserve system.[16]

The main benefit of a gold coin standard was that the people were at liberty to convert their currency to gold. It was the people that were empowered. In other words, if the nation's leaders ran irresponsible fiscal programs resulting in a depreciating currency, the people and other sovereign nations had the right to demand gold from the country's banks and treasury. The gold coin standard in essence forced fiscal prudence onto the government.

Make no mistake; the gold coin standard did not end the business cycle. Nor will it ever if the gold standard is resurrected. Some of the most serious and destructive economic downturns occurred under the gold coin standard. There were very severe recessions and depressions with high unemployment while the gold coin standard was operational in the United States.

The purpose of the gold coin standard, or the bimetallic standard the framers created, was not designed to stop the business cycle, or circumvent a laissez fare boom/bust, winner/loser contextual backdrop to the economy. Rather, bimetallism and the gold coin standard were designed to be bulwarks to shield the people and industry from government paper money monkeys run amok. The framers knew that the business cycle would endure. Their goal simply was to eliminate at least one obstructive force, namely, irresponsible government monetary policy, thus allowing the people to get on with their lives.

After the United States exited the gold coin standard in 1933 when President Roosevelt made it illegal to own

---

[16] Roy W. Jastram and Jill Leyland, The Golden Constant: The English and American Experience 1560-2007 (Northampton, MA. Edward Elgar, 2007), pp. 180-181.

gold, the monetary system transformed to a gold exchange standard. The gold exchange standard was operational until 1971, except during World War II. Operationally, the gold exchange standard was miles apart from the gold coin standard.

The gold exchange standard was designed for country to country trade balance settlements in gold. Basically, if a country began to run deficits, as the U.S. did in the 1960's, her trade partners could yank gold from the country's vaults as a correcting mechanism. It was a vote of no-confidence, if you will, on the fiscal and trade policies of the government.

In theory, once the trade and fiscal balances were back in line, gold would flow back into the country. But the key difference was that the people really didn't play a part in the grand scheme of things. This was due to the fact that under the gold exchange standard there was a huge minimum amount of currency that needed to be presented to the treasury before the cash for gold exchange could transpire. This effectively omitted all but sovereign nations and the very rich.

Summary

The Constitution did not establish a gold or silver standard. The Coinage Act of 1792 established a bimetallic standard. The Constitution defines the dollar as 371 ¼ fine grains of silver, which in turn defines gold.

The dollar is based on the Spanish milled silver dollar which was the predominant form of money in America in 1792. Congress, through the Constitution, is granted the power to coin money. Through an Act of Congress the

United States ended bimetallism in 1873. The gold standard was voted into law in 1900.

After the revolution the delegates at the Constitutional Convention in 1787 gave Congress the right in Article 1 Section 8 to coin, regulate and fix the standard of weights and measures of money. States were prohibited from emitting bills of credit, which is say print and issue their own currency. Likewise, the states were allowed only to make gold and silver coin a tender in payment of debts. The Coinage Act of 1792 defined the weights and measures of the coins.

The *dollar* was defined in the Coinage Act as 371 4/16 grains fine silver and was based on the Spanish milled silver dollar. Distilling the definition of the *dollar* even further, silver was defined in terms of gold at a ratio of 15 to 1. Thus, the framers of the Constitution created a bimetallic form of money at fixed ratios to each other. The framers were very suspicious of paper money, debated it in full at the Constitutional Convention and decisively chose a hard money currency as the best form of money for the benefit of the republic and people.

The Coin Act of 1792, as noted, established a 15:1 ratio for gold to silver. Using $1 for silver and a $1 gold eagle the bimetallic Constitutional *dollar* can be described in the following way:

371¼ Grains Silver. 24.75 Grains Gold

Chapter 5

The Origin of the Federal Reserve

The Acts of the Apostles of Fiat

The central bank is an institution of the most deadly hostility existing against the Principles and form of our Constitution. I am an Enemy to all banks discounting bills or notes for anything but Coin. If the American People allow private banks to control the issuance of their currency, first by inflation and then by deflation, the banks and corporations that will grow up around them will deprive the People of all their Property until their Children will wake up homeless on the continent their Fathers conquered.

Thomas Jefferson

The Federal Reserve System that governs banking and financial oversight in the United States originated with the Federal Reserve Act of December 23, 1913. It arose during a period of progressive legislation that started in the 1890's in response to an American economy modernizing through the growth of large corporations, improved communication, railroads, trusts, machine politics, education and globalization. Although the meaning and purpose of progressivism has changed over the years at first it was an effort to streamline business and working conditions. It was a large scale program that functioned on the notion that the good of society was best served by meeting the needs of business and industry.

Origin of the Federal Reserve

To these ends broad legislative actions were undertaken to address many of the leading issues of the day. Taken in whole these initiatives transformed the United States economy from a general system of laissez-faire to that of statist governance.[1] One of these legislative devices to which I will speak momentarily was the Federal Reserve Act shepherded cunningly through Congress by banking interests over a period of two decades. First, some background.

Under the rough and tumble laissez-faire economic system of the American economy of the late 19th century business was very competitive. Fortunes were made and lost in a survival of the fittest free-for-all. Most entrepreneurs and businessmen understood this law of the jungle for what it was, and did their best to stay competitive for survival. Others, mainly large businesses, viewed the situation differently. The goal of big business was ***political capitalism***: the utilization of political outlets to attain conditions of ***stability*** (elimination of internecine competition and erratic fluctuations in the economy), ***predictability*** (plan future economic action on the basis of fairly calculable expectations) and ***security*** (protection from the political attacks latent in any formally democratic political structure).[2]

The big business sector of the American economy was led by J.P. Morgan and Company, an enormous and powerful financial firm with strong and influential political connections. Using its influence and power J.P. Morgan

---

[1] Gabriel Kolko, The Triumph of Conservatism: A Reinterpretation of American History, 1900-1916. (London: Free Press of Glen Collier-MacMillan, 1963) 2-3.

[2] Ibid, page 3.

worked very hard to establish like-minded alliances to form cartels. The purpose was to drive out lower cost competitors and erect barriers to entry. In this fashion the cartels could control the market through pricing and obstruction for easy, consistent and reliable profits.

Morgan had help in the drive for monopoly power. Other *"important businessmen and their lawyers in the first years of this century* (early 1900's) *were convinced that big business was necessary, inevitable, and desirable as a prerequisite to rationally organizing economic life. And the destructiveness of competition and the alleged technical superiority of consolidated firms were the catalytic agents of change which made industrial cooperation and concentration a part of the "march of civilization,"* ...[3]

The First Cartels

Railroads were the first attempt at cartelization in this period of creeping progressivism, although it took some time to establish traction. Gaining control of the Albany and Susquehanna Railroad in 1869 Morgan and company began bankrolling and developing a railroad empire across the United States. Syndicates were organized by Morgan. These syndicates then purchased, leased and reorganized competing railroads.[4] Internecine rivalries from within and brutal competition from without ended this first attempt at monopoly. To protect the public from the failure of the free market and cartelization the Sherman Antitrust Act was

---

[3] Ibid, page 12.
[4] Ron Chernow, The House of Morgan: An America Dynasty and the Rise of Modern Finance (New York: Atlantic Monthly Press, 1990) Chapter 3.

passed in 1890. The goal of the Sherman Act was to stop the coupling of businesses that might impair competition.

After tremendous growth in the 1880's the business cycle began to wane in the 90's. A severe depression struck the country in 1893. As noted, the Morgan business empire had been at the center of a tremendous railroad building spree that set off widespread speculation. In some cases projects were developed with cash flow streams barely supporting expenses. Inevitably, a few of the rail projects went bankrupt, and the dam broke.[5] Project after project was iced or scuttled until economic conditions improved. The ripple effect of bankruptcy and project cancellation had a severe effect in industrialized cities. Rural and agricultural areas were no less hurt. By some measures, unemployment rose to eighteen percent. The depression that started in 1893 did not fully end until 1899.

Attempts at cartelization did not end. New and creative ways were fashioned to circumvent the Sherman Antitrust legislation. During the 1890's through the early stages of the 20th century the steel industry, for example, came under the wistful eye of the monopolists. This attempt failed as well from intense competition despite a high tariff wall designed to protect American industry, and keep out lower cost foreign goods.

Big business shifted gears at this point, and this is where the rubber meets the road. Rather than working through their own initiative with like-minded businessmen the budding monopolists decided to use the levers of government to protect their turf from competition and the

---

[5] The Reading Railroad and the Union Pacific Railway are two examples.

free market. The task would be to alter the makeup of the America economy from a laissez-faire system to statist bureaucracy. In what may be called regulatory capture the big business interests successfully lobbied and wrought control of the regulatory bureaucracies by employing their own people at the various agencies.

Nice dividends soon were paid. Working with the intellectual community big business interests were able to propagandize the American people into accepting greater government control of the economy - for the greater good of society, of course - and higher wages for the benefit of all.

Naturally, with regulatory capture, big business was able to protect their turf from the free market by using insiders to write favorable legislation enacting subsidies and various restrictions to pad profits. The academic world, as noted, climbed aboard the monopoly bandwagon, too, although they paid lip service to a belief in laissez faire economic theory. True, differences arose between big business, politicians, the government and the academy. But on the fundamental doctrine that big business combinations were good for society and that *"ruinous competition"* must be avoided at all costs all were in agreement. In but twenty years there had been a wholesale change in attitude and perspective.

The Rich Man's Panic of 1907

In the meantime, no sooner had the economy recovered from the depression of the 1890's when a crisis walloped the stock market – the so-called rich man's panic of 1907. In actuality, the panic of 1907 was one of a series of crises that smacked the banking system in the years after the civil war. Eight panics had thumped the economy and the markets since 1873. The rich man's panic would be the ninth.[6] One might conclude that the 1907 panic was nothing new or unusual. And it wasn't. It just so happened that the 1907 panic was one of the worst, and it came at a time when the winds of reform were blowing favorably for change. The panic of 1907 thus became the casus belli for the creation of the Federal Reserve.

The panic of 1907 actually was *"triggered by the literal and figurative shock of a massive earthquake and a rash of fires that destroyed the city of San Francisco in (April) 1906 ..."*[7] The damage from the earthquake and the fires did tremendous damage not only to San Francisco but to the United States as well. Upon news of the quake stocks in New York sold off 12%. Over the next year and a half a *"series of major market downturns, culminating in a 37 percent decline in the value of all listed stocks"* would strike Wall Street.[8]

The zenith of the panic of 1907 arrived in October of that year. It began innocently enough with an attempt by a few greedy adventurers to corner the market in a copper company called United Copper. The plan was pretty straight forward. Take a big position, employ leverage, drive the stock up through rumors of a takeover in speculative frenzy and force the shorts to cover, or buy, which drives the stock higher still. Using the vernacular of Wall Street the action in United Copper was a bear squeeze.

---

[6] From the National Bureau of Economic Research.
[7] Robert F. Bruner and Sean D. Carr, The Panic of 1907: Lessons Learned from the Market's Perfect Storm (Hoboken, NJ: John Wiley & Sons, 2007), pp. 2-3.
[8] Ibid, page 13.

Unfortunately for the swashbucklers the short squeeze went terribly wrong. As it happened, they were too undercapitalized to pull off the squeeze, although at first the gambit looked promising as United Copper climbed from $38 to $62. When word circulated that the players held a weak hand speculators smelled blood in the water. The shorts did not capitulate. Rather, they doubled down much to the dismay of the United Copper manipulators. Others, sensing an ideal opportunity to exit the stock with a nice profit, sold into the rally, and exited with their winnings. At lightening pace the market then turned against the owners of the concentrated, leveraged position in United Copper. Within days United Copper plunged to $10 per share, wiping out the players of the scheme, who were leveraged to the gills.[9]

This might have served poetic justice to the schemers had the fallout been limited to them. But it wasn't. Panic surged into the broader market, and started to pull all boats down in the suction of the sinking short squeeze. This led to a run on the Knickerbocker Trust Company, whose President, Charles Barney, was thought to have participated preeminently in the scheme, losing Trust money in the process. When word spread that Knickerbocker checks were not being accepted by other institutions panic ensued. Within days the Knickerbocker Trust ceased operations as frightened depositors aggressively pulled their money from the bank. Several other big name financial companies failed, or came close to failing, as well. Panic, contagion and leverage had struck again.

---

[9] Ibid, Chapter 6.

Origin of the Federal Reserve

Before it was over stocks had dropped roughly fifty per percent from their 1906 peak. Confidence was severely shaken. But for the banking interests the 1907 panic was the perfect narrative to appeal for change. The banking elite immediately seized the moment and coalesced around the idea that new banking conventions had to be developed. This led to the formation of the National Monetary Commission in 1908 spearheaded by Senator Nelson W. Aldrich. Together with other members of the Senate and House of Representatives the commission was charged with 1) conducting a broad study of the banking system, 2) the causes of the banking crises affecting the banking system since the civil war and 3) alternatives and solutions to improve the system. The commission was stacked with bankers.

There was little doubt the commission members wanted a central bank. What the members really coveted, however, was an *elastic currency,* and for three basic reasons. First, the commissioners wanted the ability to expand the money supply when business conditions slowed, or tighten when business expanded above trend. Second, they wanted to be able to prevent price deflation. Third, the commissioners wanted to keep prices stable. The party line was that an *elastic currency* provided all these benefits and served the public interest because it controlled the animal spirits of bankers seeking profits.

Yet the need behind the need for an *elastic currency* had deeper roots. The bankers wanted to use it as an instrument to defeat the business cycle once and forever. Having a central bank at the ready to backstop bad loans was an added feature. This would allow the banks to loan with greater latitude knowing that a central bank stood behind them to bail them out when loans failed. Typically, this happened then, as today, at the end of an expansion. The problem was that the banks back in the day had to liquidate loans at fire sale prices, which is to say, at a loss. But with a central bank, the reputed lender of last resort, they would have an able ally that would loan them money, or inflate, and therefore circumvent the messy need to call in loans. In other words, profits for bankers now and forever. This was the proverbial need behind the need.

Once the National Monetary Commission got its bearings straight the members embarked on a grand tour of Europe. The purpose was to study the leading banking institutions, harvest the best ideas and implement them in the United States. To appeal to public sensibilities the Commissioners and the banking elite promised that any changes would benefit the public interest. Of course, this was all political theater. As expected, once the commission released its report it contained a proposal to create a National Reserve Association to be regulated, ruled and controlled by the banking industry. The ruse immediately was recognized and greeted with pronounced suspicion. It went nowhere with the public.

The Federal Reserve is Formed

The bankers were determined to have their way. For the next few years they maneuvered and schemed behind closed doors in the halls of Congress. Finally, in 1913 they were able to move a bill through both legislative branches that President Wilson agreed to sign. The resulting Federal Reserve Act created Federal Reserve Banks which would provide an *elastic currency*, which was a fancy way to say it would inflate the money supply as necessary. To be exact the legislation called for *"the establishment of the Federal Reserve banks, to furnish an elastic currency, to afford means of rediscounting commercial paper and to establish a more effective supervision of banking in the United States, and for other purposes."*[10]

Thus, at long last, the banking establishment successfully propagandized and wore down the public and their leaders until they finally got their coveted central bank and mandate for an *elastic currency.* In reality, the Federal Reserve Act gave the Fed monopoly power over the creation of money, and the ability to inflate and deflate the currency of the United States with impunity. *Cui bono?*

Fractional Reserve Banking: A Brief Primer

One of the ways the Fed uses the *elastic currency* to control the money supply is through fractional reserve banking. Without going into too much detail the following is the basic framework of fractional reserve banking.

Since bank depositors rarely want or need all their cash at once, fractional reserve banking allows the banks to lend out a large percentage of the depositor's money to generate interest on loans, and profit for the bank. The money that is not loaned out is called the reserve. The Federal Reserve can adjust the reserve ratio up or down depending on business conditions. For example if the economy slows the Fed can lower the reserve ratio which allows the banks to make loans and stimulate production and demand. Or if the economy starts growing too fast the Fed can increase the reserve ratio thus slowing the economy back

---

[10] This quote is the full title of the act passed by Congress. "An Act to provide for the establishment ..."

to a more reasonable rate of growth. This sounds good on the surface, but the devil is in the details.

The problem with fractional reserve banking arises when the bank makes bad loans. If the depositors of the bank catch wind that the bank has made bad loans they naturally want their money. So if a large number of depositors go to the bank and demand their money there's trouble. Since the bank has loaned out the bulk of the depositor's money the bank has only a fraction of that money on hand. The bank cannot meet the demand of the depositors. This has happened throughout history. The bank thus has the choice of either borrowing money, selling assets or calling in loans to meet depositor demands. In our day the taxpayer picks up the tab if the bank fails, which they often do[11].

In a just world regulators would require that the bankers themselves pay the depositors out of their own pocketbook since it was they who lost the money. In such a world bankers would be certain to practice extremely tough due diligence before they loaned out depositor money. Indeed, the bankers would loan out the money as if it were their own, which in a way it is if they would have to pay back the depositors if there wasn't enough cash on hand to meet demand. But with fractional reserve banking as it exists today in the United States you have the exact opposite. The bankers have an accommodative central bank, deposit insurance and an elastic currency at their disposal. This system allows bankers extreme latitude to make loans for fun and profit without personal accountability.

---

[11] In modern times the Fed uses open market operations to control the money supply more often than adjusting the required reserve ratio.

Performance Review[12]

So how has the Federal Reserve performed in the past one hundred years? Let us take a brief survey of the performance results.

Using the Federal Reserve's own interpretation to its mission it has failed. The results are self-evident. Performance measurements and statistics show the abject failure. Admittedly, the banking system prior to the creation of the Federal Reserve was far from perfect. But the less than perfect system preceding it doesn't excuse the failed performance metrics of the Fed since 1913.

The mission of the Federal Reserve in general is 1) *"conducting the nation's monetary policy by influencing the monetary and credit conditions in the economy in pursuit of maximum employment, stable prices, and moderate long-term interest rates;"* and 2) to *"ensure the safety and soundness of the nation's banking and financial system."*[13]

Let's review the results that the Fed has established for itself.

How well has the Fed performed in stabilizing employment? Studying the 1930's, 1970's, 1980's and the first decade of the 21st century clearly proves that the level of unemployment under Federal Reserve "scientific management" is no better than it was before the Fed. Fed apologists like to point to modern day globalism and offshoring of jobs as a reason for elevated unemployment.

---

[12] George Selgin, William Lastrapes, Lawrence White, "Has the Fed Been a Failure?" Cato Working Paper Dec. 2010.
[13] Citation: http://www.federalreserve.gov/aboutthefed/mission.htm

Origin of the Federal Reserve

But globalism is not new. Globalism existed before the Federal Reserve came onto the scene.

The record is clear, decisively so: the period between 1879 and 1914, the high point of the international gold standard, the world was experiencing tremendous worldwide capital flows on a scale unprecedented in history. During this period the world experienced a tremendous burst of prosperity and peace. Indeed, the magnitude of the flow of trade, investment and job creation was so large that world leaders were wont to believe World War I would prove to be a short lived affair due to the interconnection of the major powers. It was believed that, because all players would lose economically in a destructive war, sensible government and industry leaders would quickly intercede to stop a huge conflagration since everybody would lose, and nobody gain. Of course, this did not happen. A devastating world war erupted. But the point is that globalism is not a new phenomenon. So the Fed cannot say that it is globalism that has caused their stewardship to wane versus the pre-Fed period.[14]

How has the Federal Reserve performed in maintaining price stability of goods and services in the economy? This is polite company so I'll simply say Fed performance in this category is miserable. The loss of purchasing power of the dollar since 1913 is terrible. It takes roughly $22.70 to buy what cost a dollar in 1913. For those keeping score that represents a 2,270% percent increase.[15]

---

[14] See *The Great Illusion* written by Normal Angell in 1910 and Barbara Tuchman's *The Guns of August* written in 1962 for a flavor of the peace and prosperity of the pre-World War I times.
[15] From the Bureau of Labor Statistics.

Origin of the Federal Reserve

Indeed, from virtually day one the Federal Reserve instituted a policy of inflation.[16]

Almost the moment the United States entered World War I in 1917 the Fed started monetizing[17] the Treasury's debt and manipulating interest rates to lower the debt servicing costs of the Treasury. In the process the rate of inflation soared. The inflation rate in some quarters of the war annualized at a rate close to 40%. The wartime embargo on the export of gold may have factored into some of the increase; but not all of it. However, there's an interesting point to note. At the point when the Fed was no longer constrained by the gold standard the rate of inflation and money printing went into overdrive. Stated yet another way, it was the gold standard that shackled the Fed from printing money, raising the inflation rate and destroying the dollar.

Keep in mind that from 1790 until 1913 the rise in consumer prices was up roughly 8%.[18] True, these are rough and ready numbers. But since 1913 when the Federal Reserve was tossed the keys by Congress to run monetary policy money creation is up 12,000%. The debate is not even competitive. Federal Reserve price stability performance measurements compared to the pre-Fed period loses huge,

---

[16] See the Index of Wholesale Commodity Prices: Page 240-241. Minority Report of the United States Gold Commission to the House of Representatives and to the Senate, March 31, 1982.
[17] Monetizing is the mechanism of converting U.S. government debt (bonds) into cash so the government has cash to spend.
[18] H. R. Hodges, Economic Conditions: 1815 – 1914 (London: George Allen & Unwin, 1917). The dollar was the same rate to the pound in 1830 as in 1914 due to the fact currencies were pegged to gold. Deflation (the good kind from productivity gains) rather than inflation was the rule in the 19th century rather than inflation that existed in the 20th century. The 19th century was a century of currency and price stability.

even taking into consideration a lousy banking system prior to 1913.

How good a job has the Federal Reserve done in the predictability of inflation? Let's take a look. As early as the 13th century the city states of Italy first issued perpetual bonds - bonds with no maturity. In the western world this practice gained a foothold and continued through the 19th century under the stability of the gold standard. However, perpetual bond issuance ceased after World War I because of high rates and the instability of the bond market sans the gold standard.

How about deflation under Federal Reserve? There are basically two types of deflation. One type of deflation is good. That's the deflation from innovation, productivity gains and product improvement: think computers. The 19th century was a century of deflation, the good kind, owing to productivity gains, product improvement and innovation. The second type of deflation is the scary type. This is the deflation of the 1930's when the velocity of money assumes the fetal position, and prices tumble from liquidation and demand decreases regardless of price.

Under the current Federal Reserve System in the United States the people have had to endure recurring periods of severe deflation only to be followed by severe periods of inflation under the poor leadership of the apostles of fiat. The people have had to endure the bad deflation of 1921, the 1930's and the severe deflation starting in 2008. These periods were crossed by severe periods of inflation during World War I, the mid 1940's and the 1960's and 70's.

Origin of the Federal Reserve

Demonstrably, the Federal Reserve impoverishes the American people with the scary type of deflation; but they make up for this flaw by goring the people with severe periods of inflation to offset deflation. A cynic might presume this is the Fed's way of staying relevant.

With this in mind, take a second look at Thomas Jefferson's famous warning posted at the beginning of this chapter. When one looks closely at the performance of the Federal Reserve the evidence is conclusive that Jefferson knew exactly what he was talking about. Central banks, without the forced discipline of the gold standard, continually whipsaw the people from one extreme of deflation to the other extreme of inflation. Maybe that's why Jefferson was one of the founding fathers of the country. He was a smart guy.

Deliberating yet another performance measurement, how well has the Federal Reserve performed in stopping financial panics during its watch? Unsurprisingly, not well at all. Thousands and thousands of banks failed in the great depression between 1929 and 1933. The number of bank failures stopped only when the taxpayer began to back the deposits of the banks through the good offices of the FDIC. In other words, it wasn't Fed supervision, oversight or "scientific management" that stopped bank failures. It was taxpayer backstop.[19]

But even given taxpayer backing bank failures have not stopped, nor have the financial panics. There have been serious bank failures from the 1970's through our current

---

[19] As noted, for a superb, detailed analysis of the performance of the Fed see George Selgin, William Lastrapes, Lawrence White, "Has the Fed Been a Failure?" Cato Working Paper Dec. 2010.

day. In Texas in the 1980's, for example, all of the big banks in the state essentially failed during the oil bust, and were taken over by the "money center" banks of the day as they were called. And, of course, there was the savings and loan crisis of the 1980's and the financial panic starting in 2008.

Now it's true the Federal Reserve doesn't regulate savings and loans.[20] But Federal Reserve officials, their acolytes and apologists have told us they're the smartest guys in the room. Therefore, we the people have every right to expect the men from Mensa to do what they told us they could do if given control over the nation's monetary policy. Instead, we've been saddled with something quite the opposite. The people have had to endure the continual whipsawing back and forth of inflation and deflation because of Fed mismanagement. Indeed, Fed bungling has created a veritable primordial soup for the development of panics and bubbles.

Continuing onward, how well has the Federal Reserve performed in smoothing out the peaks and valleys of the business cycle? Again, not well at all. According to one economic study, "recessions have not become noticeably shorter over time. The average length of recessions is actually one month longer in the post-World War II era than in the pre-World War I era."[21]

In fairness to the Fed, the same study shows that the length of expansions has been noticeably longer. Yet it was a few very long expansions that skewed the data. At the same

---

[20] The Office of Thrift Supervision regulates federally-chartered savings and loans and federal savings banks.
[21] Christina D. Romer, Journal of Economic Perspectives—Volume 13, Number 2—Spring 1999—Pages 23-44. See page 30 for key points.

time, since this report was issued in 1999, the United States economy has experienced two very nasty recessions, one in 2001 after the dot com NASDAQ bubble burst, and the very severe panic of 2008 when the whole system seemed about to blow. In between these two severe downturns was the real estate bubble. So in the span of less than a decade the people have had to suffer the consequences of our forefather's not heeding Jefferson's advice not once, or twice, but three times.

Summary

The Federal Reserve System was created with the expressed intent to inflate an elastic currency.

In summation, what all this means in plain English is that the Federal Reserve has not lived up to its billing as a reason for its existence. We were told when the Fed was organized that if they got their coveted elastic currency the smartest guys in the room would smooth out the business cycle, and financial panics would be put to rest. Only now, with hard evidence slapping everybody in the face, Federal Reserve officials and apologists are falling back on the excuse that while they aren't able to stop panics, the panics themselves would have been much worse if the Fed hadn't been around to act. The past is prologue; expect more of the same going forward, unless the beast is put to death.

The Federal Reserve System

Born to Inflate: Guaranteed to Deflate

Chapter 6

1933

Default

Default is the failure to live up to the terms of a contract. It is the breach of a covenant. In 1933 the United States government broke a covenant with the people of the United States when it ended the pledge to exchange dollars for gold on demand. This was a dollar default.

Life in the United States in 1932 was grim. The unemployment rate was closing in on 25% at a time when women were not a big component in the labor force. Farm prices had been cut in half. Thirteen million people had lost their jobs since the crash of the stock market in 1929. Gross national product had fallen by a third. International trade had plummeted by two-thirds. Ten thousand banks had failed. Industrial stocks on the exchanges had lost eighty percent of their value. At the time, the economic downturn had yet to be called "The Great Depression." But by 1932 everybody knew in retrospect that an earth-shattering downturn had engulfed the country since 1929.

1932 also was a presidential election year. The race was between Democrat Franklin D. Roosevelt and the incumbent, Republican Herbert Hoover.

1933

In his acceptance speech in Chicago at the Democrat National Convention Roosevelt pledged a New Deal for the American people. The New Deal later came to be called the three r's: relief, reform and recovery. On the stump Roosevelt campaigned on a platform of a "federal budget annually balanced", a revenue generating tariff, banking and financial reform, support for veteran's pensions, aid for farmers, spending cuts, "the rehabilitation of silver"[1] and a "sound currency to be preserved at all hazards." Regarding this latter no mention of adherence to the gold standard was mentioned.

Hoover wanted to stay the course. The Republican campaign called for substantial reductions in federal spending, the maintenance of the protective tariff, the continuance of the gold standard, restrictions on immigration and appeals for voluntarism to solve the economic problems of the United States.

Given the economic climate Hoover was dispatched with extreme prejudice. After the election the Democrats, led by Roosevelt, controlled both houses of Congress by wide margins.

From Election Day on November 8, 1932 until the inauguration day on March 4, 1933 stood a long four months. During the November to March interval some observers of the political spectrum began to take notice of a few of Roosevelt's advisors. These men seemed to embrace radical and unconventional political and economic ideas.

---

[1] The United States had been on the gold standard since 1879. Expressing the will of several special interest groups many politicians had agitated for the return of the free coinage of silver. The movement had died out after the establishment of the Fed.

Particularly concerning was the possibility of these advisors recommending Roosevelt take the United States off the gold standard coupled with a devaluation of the dollar. Some Americans already were concerned before Roosevelt assumed office with this potential calamity. During the Presidential campaign Hoover mentioned in a speech that in November 1931 the government had thought seriously about ending the gold standard as the banking and economic crisis had deepened.

In late 1932 and early 1933 banks still were closing. Almost 300 banks closed the last quarter of 1932. In January 1933, 249 banks closed. By the end of February twenty four states had closed their banks to one degree or another. Given this environment, with talk of currency devaluation and rumors swirling about a national banking holiday on top of the state banking holidays already standing, U.S. citizens took action. Foreigners did too. Both groups began to withdraw money from circulation, redeem cash for gold and in many instances ship gold out of the country.

February – March 4, 1933

As Roosevelt's inauguration drew nearer the redemption of dollars to gold quickened. In February 1933, a month before Roosevelt took office, the gold stock in banks fell by more than $170 million as worried depositors, both domestic and foreign, converted their dollars to gold coin and bullion. Money in circulation increased by more than $800 million during this period, an increase of 16%, as depositors withdrew cash from banks. These actions alarmed banking and treasury officials.

1933

The trend would continue. On March 3, 1933, the day before Roosevelt's inauguration, gold outflow from the banking system became acute. That single day saw $200 million in gold exit from the Federal Reserve Bank of New York. $150 million in currency was pulled as well. $100 million in gold was redeemed from member banks in Chicago. The speed of redemption of currency into gold, then priced at $20.67 per ounce, and the liquidation of bank reserves was stunning. Federal Reserve officials were quite startled. Money was flying out of the banks and the country at an alarming rate.[2]

Lost in the chaos was one key dynamic: the money leaving the banking system belonged to the people, not the banks, the Federal Reserve or the government. The people preferred gold based on what they perceived to be future government policy decisions. This dynamic was the expressed purpose of the gold standard. The framers had instituted a hard money monetary system so the people might protect themselves from government deprivations of paper money.[3] Thus when the people perceived that the government was planning an inflationary recourse to solve the economic problems of the depression, they acted. The people took possession of gold as was their right. On the front of every dollar in their wallet was printed the following clause:

---

[2] Francis G. Awalt, Recollections of the Banking Crisis in 1933, from a History of the Federal Reserve: Volume 1: 1913-1951. 358 pp. (Source: St. Louis Federal Reserve. Business History Review, 43, Autumn, 1969: pp. 347-371)

[3] The framers envisioned a self-correcting policy. The people would keep the banks and government honest when they spotted shady dealings. The people would pull their money from the banks and the treasury, who then would be forced to reverse policy to attract gold back.

1933

"Redeemable in gold on demand at the United States Treasury, or in gold or lawful money at any Federal Reserve Bank."

The people accepted this fact at face value. Redeeming cash for gold was an accepted fact of life even if for convenience one carried cash. But as the banking crisis mounted more and more people thought twice about holding cash, either in their checking accounts at shaky banks, or in actual cash that could be devalued. Thus, they redeemed. So fast had the money left the banking system and country that many observers believed a national banking holiday was the only route to avoid national bankruptcy.

In any event, the people were well founded in their distrust of the banks. The fact remained that a good amount of the loans the banks had made were in default. For example, a huge number of farm loans made by banks were worthless. The collapse in commodity prices from overproduction had created severe strain for farmers to pay back the principal and interest on their loans. Many depositors knew the score, too, because they were the very people in hock to the bank, as were their friends and neighbors in the farming community. Thus, the people had a very real concern about leaving their money in a bank that might fail. Keep in mind; this is the period before bank deposit insurance. If a bank in which you had your money failed, you lost your money. Such a tendency tended to focus one's attention to the details of the bank's strength.

Still, farmers did the best they could. In a few states mortgage moratoriums were enacted. But given the dire straight of farming few were willing to buy a farm, whether directly from a farmer or from a bank liquidation. Large swaths of bank assets thus had limited value. In addition, as gold left the country or went under the mattress, less collateral was available for bank loans.

At the time, the gold standard included a requirement that the money supply in the United States have a backing of 40% gold. So as prudent savers pulled cash from banks, or redeemed cash for gold, officials in Washington and bankers accused them of *"hoarding"* gold. *"Traitorous hoarding"* it was called. These people were hurting the country it was said.

Despite the accusations and demonization of so-called gold *"hoarders"* people tend to act in their own best interests. The decision thus to legally redeem dollars for gold became an easy one when reasoning that while today one might pay $20.67 for an ounce of gold, tomorrow one might have to pony up $25, or $30. As events later were to prove the *"traitorous hoarders"* were right.

Adding to the panic was the amount of gold on hand. Roosevelt rightly pointed out in his fireside chat on May 7, 1933, the amount of gold in the whole world amounted to roughly $11 billion. The United States owned $4 billion or so of this amount. Yet the obligations payable in gold by the United States government and private industry ran to upwards of $100 billion. This discrepancy was not lost on either the public or foreign interests. Those who knew the numbers chose to act decisively. Simply stated, if you wanted to get your gold you had better be the first one in line because, if there were a run on gold at the banks, you might not get any.

1933

Background: Banking Holiday

The goals of those proposing a national banking holiday were several-fold. Primarily the need was for bank examiners to have time to review the financial statements of the banks, and decide which banks were solvent and which ones weren't. A second goal was to buy time to print more currency to give to banks to meet customer demand. Once the examination process was completed the plan was for the Federal Reserve to provide currency to the solvent banks and issue loans against bank assets. At that point solvent banks would be reopened with cash on hand for customers to withdraw. Word would spread that the crisis was over. Confidence and trust would be restored. The banking system would be saved.

It was a sensible plan given the environment. However, there still remained the thorny issue of currency debasement. If the bankers, regulators and government wanted to attract gold and cash back to the banks they needed to restore credibility with the people. They had to prove they had no intentions of debasing the dollar, or ending the gold standard; they also needed to prove the banking system was strong. Yet all this needed to be done in the midst of an ongoing systemic banking collapse. The undeniable fact was that many of the banks already were closed due to widespread pre-existing banking holidays created at the state level. Roosevelt made this clear when he pointed this out in his foreside chat on March 12, 1933:

"By the afternoon of March 3d scarcely a bank in the country was open to do business. Proclamations temporarily closing them, in whole or part, had been issued by the Governors in almost all the States."

1933

So what to do?

The Trading with the Enemy Act of 1917

The 1917 Trading with the Enemy Act was the prescribed legal remedy to the problem. A clause within the act allowed the president to close the banks and stop the withdrawal of gold out of the banks whether by domestic or foreign depositors. The primary difficulty was that this law, passed during World War I, was designed to be used by the President in times of war which most assuredly the United States was not in at the time. A second problem was that the Trading with the Enemy Act had been amended just prior to the end of World War I. In this amendment the act was slated to end two years after the cessation of hostilities. World War I ended in November 1918. Thus the act had been dead for over a decade. A third problem was that the Constitution did not permit the Congress to ban gold transactions. Nor did the Constitution allow Congress, which had oversight of the people's money, to transfer oversight to another governmental branch such as the Executive Office of the President.

Yet possibly the most disconcerting aspect of using the Trading with the Enemy Act was the provision criminalizing dealing in gold.[4] The United States was not at war. And by withdrawing cash from shaky banks, or converting their dollars to gold, the people were acting in their own best interests. Indeed, these were the very tools the framers had conjured for the people. It was a means to protect the people from debasement, and to keep government honest.

---

[4] Ten years in prison and/or $10,000 fine.

1933

Understanding the constitutional issues, President Hoover had been reluctant to use the Trading with the Enemy Act as a tool in declaring a national banking holiday. Despite his reservations, and out of desperation, Hoover did float the idea with Roosevelt on the eve of the inauguration. The proposal was to issue a proclamation closing the banks for a while so things could be sorted out using the Trading with the Enemy Act as legal cover. Roosevelt refused to take action until his inauguration. Yet Roosevelt had every intention of doing exactly what Hoover proposed, namely, to issue a proclamation using the Trading with the Enemy Act as justification to close the banks. Hoover, thus, was left twisting in the wind.

The truth is that the hour was too late for Hoover to do anything on a national level. His credibility was shot. Regardless, the Senate had adjourned. Therefore, there was no chance of an emergency proclamation via a joint Congressional resolution with the House of Representatives. It thus fell upon the Hoover administration, the Federal Reserve and Treasury officials to persuade the state governors to call for a bank holiday at the state level to stop the outflow of currency and gold from the banks, and save the country from insolvency.

As one can imagine matters were quite rushed. Working through the night of March 3, 1933, in one of the last acts of the Hoover administration, officials of the Federal government were able to persuade the governors of New York, Pennsylvania, Illinois, Massachusetts and New Jersey among other states to declare banking holidays at the state level. Given that March 4, 1933 was a Saturday most banks in the country were closed as a matter practice. Banks in Washington D.C. were closed because of Inauguration

1933

Day. Some Federal Reserve Banks were closed as well although the Cleveland Fed remained open.[5] The Dallas Fed did too. Dallas closed though when it got a call from a depositor in Pittsburgh stating that an airplane was in route to withdraw ten million dollars.[6] Thus was the state of affairs in the United States on the eve of Roosevelt's inauguration.

Proclamations and Decrees

At noon on March 4, 1933 Roosevelt was inaugurated. The greatest applause during his inaugural address came when he said that in the event Congress failed to take bold action he would ask for *"broad Executive power to wage a war against the emergency, as great as the power that would be given to me if we were in fact invaded by a foreign foe."* This was language cleverly designed to prepare the public that strong measures were coming. It also was designed to tip off public officials that the wartime Trading with the Enemy Act was to be resurrected to wage war against *"traitorous hoarders"* of gold.

Upon completion of the inaugural address members of the Roosevelt administration, Treasury, Federal Reserve, Congress and the banking sector huddled to sort out the details of the banking holiday. In the meantime, Roosevelt issued Proclamation 2038[7] calling on Congress to *"convene in extra session at twelve o'clock, noon, on the Ninth day of March, 1933, to receive such communication as may be made by the Executive."*[8] This was on Sunday March 5, 1933.

---

[5] Awalt, 360.
[6] St. Louis Federal Reserve Internal Memorandum and Interview with Joseph P. Dreibelbis, an outside counsel to the Federal Reserve.
[7] See Index for full text of the Proclamation.
[8] Proclamation 2038 signed March 5, 1933. See Index.

1933

With so much uncertainty in the air it was clear that something had to be done. A vague plan emerged. Despite the nebulous Constitutional authority vested in the Trading with the Enemy Act the Roosevelt team decided to press forward.

A consensus emerged. Banking was a nationwide problem.[9] The solution thus had to be nationwide. In that vein all the banks would be on the same footing with a national plan of action. Therefore, a holiday would be declared. The banks would be examined. Insolvent banks would be closed. Staggered openings then would resume at the end of the holiday, and things would return to normal.[10]

The Banking Holiday

Proclamation 2039[11] was drafted declaring a national banking holiday effective from March 4, 1933 through March 9, 1933. Roosevelt signed the proclamation on March 6, and the banking holiday took effect, essentially stopping all banking transactions until the deadline passed on March 9, 1933.

In Proclamation 2039 Roosevelt stated that the country was in a *"national emergency."* The national emergency he said was because of the *"unwarranted"* withdrawals of gold and currency from the nation's banking system strictly for the purpose of *"hoarding."* Gold removed by foreign interests for *"speculative activity"* also had led to the depletion of the gold capital of the country. The nation

---

[9] St. Louis Federal Reserve: Joseph P. Dreibelbis said the banking problem lay with corporate wire transfers, not public withdrawals: March 9, 1954 interview.
[10] Awalt, 361.
[11] Proclamation 2039 signed March 6, 1933. See Appendix.

1933

and the people had been hurt, Roosevelt said. The *"hoarding"* had to stop. *"Appropriate measures"* would be undertaken *"to protect the interests of our people."* In other words, rather than blame the banks for making bad loans, he rested the blame on the American people for exercising due diligence, and taking action to protect their hard earned money.

As noted, the legal justification for the President to close the banks was flimsy at best. Banks were private institutions. Proclamation 2039 referred to *"the Act of October 6, 1917"* but was careful not to mention the official name of the Act, lest the public become aware that they in fact were the enemy of the administration. The proclamation spoke of a *"national emergency."* But a *"national emergency"* is not necessarily war, which might have lent legal justification for Roosevelt to act as Commander-in-Chief under the "war powers"[12] section of the Constitution to protect the country from gold departing the country. So closing the banks was based on very shady legal foundation.

Regardless of the rationale for closing the banks, these were dark, rough days for the American people. Without access to their money the people had little recourse but to plunge ahead and make the best of a terrible situation.

The Emergency Banking Relief Act of March 9, 1933

It's important to understand what was happening. The banks were slated to open Friday morning March 10, 1933. Nothing banking related, short of the holiday, had changed since March 4 to address the problem. Virtually every bank in the country had been closed for six days, many

---

[12] Article II, Section 2, Clause 1 of the Constitution.

1933

longer. The American people were anxious. People needed money to eat, pay rent and meet their obligations. Likewise for businesses: payroll had to be met, supplies bought and vendors paid. Yet here it was Thursday noon, March 9, 1933 and basically nothing had changed since March 3. So there was every expectation that once the banks could legally open their doors on March 10 that gold and currency, short of some game-changing event, would resume flying out of the vaults of the banks. Roosevelt's plan was to solve the problem with new banking legislation. This was the Emergency Banking Relief Act.

As it happened, Roosevelt gathered into conference members of the House and Senate on Wednesday night March 8, 1933. The particulars of the bill were discussed. The bill had been written by Walter Wyatt, general counsel of the Federal Reserve, who had met with Roosevelt and members of his administration earlier in the week. Although Roosevelt had a list of items he wanted drafted in the bill Wyatt said he was shocked at how unprepared the Roosevelt *"Brains Trust"* was to deal with the banking crisis:

"I was absolutely amazed. There wasn't anybody in that entire Brains Trust, apparently, that had given any thought – they certainly had no plans – or any real study to the problem created by this banking situation."[13]

Or stated another way, the *"Brains Trust"* was making it up as they went along. Yet the Roosevelt administration was determined on one account: pass the bill as quickly as possible. No amendments were to be allowed to

---

[13] Anthony J. Badger, FDR: The First Hundred Days (New York, NY: Hill and Wang, A Division of Farrar, Straus and Giroux, 2008), p. 35 paperback edition.

the bill. Nor would the bill be allowed to be reviewed, examined and discussed by the House and Senate Banking and Currency Committees as customary. Nor would there be copies for members to read and examine. There was only one copy of the bill, and it was a cut and paste job. The bill would be read aloud in the chambers. No roll call vote was to be allowed in the House. A voice vote would suffice. Speed was essential. The bill needed to be passed in the House and sent to the Senate as quickly as possible. The Senate needed to do its part as well: limit the debate and get it passed for the President to sign. Then get the word out to the people through the press that the new Congress and President were taking strong measures to solve the banking problem.

March 9, 1933 Extra Session in the House and Senate

The gavel banged in the House and Senate at noon March 9, 1933, opening the extra session called by Roosevelt in his March 5, 1933 proclamation. A message from Roosevelt was conveyed. What he wanted was *"immediate enactment of legislation giving to the executive branch of the Government control over banks ..."* He also asked for amendment of the Federal Reserve Act so that the Fed might print enough paper money to meet all currency demands in the chance there might be a run on the banks.

At this point, the Emergency Banking Relief Act was introduced in the House, H.R. 1491 by number. Forty minutes of debate were granted, 20 minutes for the Democrats and 20 minutes for the Republicans. There was only one bill available and it in rough draft form at the Speaker's desk. Members of the House had to sit quietly and listen intently to what was in the bill as it was read aloud in the chamber.

1933

The whole process was more becoming a banana republic than a mature constitutional republic. Outspoken members knew it, too. Republican Representative Louis T. McFadden of Pennsylvania said:

"The first opportunity I had to know what this legislation is was when it was read from the clerk's desk ... It is a dictatorship over finance in the United States."[14]

Others expressed similar astonishment. Representative Ernest Lundeen of Minnesota summed up the situation:

"The author of this bill seems to be unknown. No one has told us who drafted the bill. There appears to be a printed copy at the Speaker's desk, but no printed copies are available for the House Members. The bill has been driven through the House with cyclonic speed after 40 minutes' debate, 20 minutes for the minority and 20 minutes for the majority. I have demanded a roll call, but have been unable to get the attention of the Chair ... we therefore have the spectacle of the great House of Representatives of the United States of America passing, after a 40 minute debate, a bill its members never read and never saw, a bill whose author is unknown ... It is safe to say that in normal times, after careful study of a printed copy and after careful debate and consideration, this bill would never have passed the House or any other House. Its passage could be accomplished only by rapid procedure, hurried and hectic debate, and a general rush for voting without roll call."[15]

---

[14] 1933 Congressional Record, 77th Congress. Page 80.
[15] 1933 Congressional Record, 77th Congress. Page 83.

1933

In other words, the bill was railroaded through the House with a voice vote. Yet, in fairness, the voice vote was more to speed up the process than anything else. With Roosevelt's huge mandate from the election, and the Democrat party in firm control of the House, there was little doubt that even with a roll call the bill would have passed easily. It's equally true that some if not all of the leadership of the Republican party were in favor of passing the bill as well, although most would confess the process of passing the bill without allowing for debate or amendments stunk to high heaven.

Late in the afternoon of March 9, 1933 the Senate took up discussion of the Emergency Banking Relief Act.[16] The situation in the world's greatest deliberative body was the same as in the House of Representatives. Senators had been coached by Roosevelt to limit debate of the bill, refuse amendments and get it passed as quickly as possible. They did not disappoint. What debate that did take place centered mainly between Senator Huey Long of Louisiana, Senator Carter Glass of Virginia and a few others over whether the bill would close permanently some 14,000 state banks and 900 national banks. It was political theater. The bill passed 73 to 7. By seven-thirty in the evening the Senate had concluded the proceedings and sent the bill to the President for signing.

Reading the bill is interesting.[17] Section 1 essentially legalized after the fact the steps taken by Roosevelt to

---

[16] St. Louis Fed: Internal Memorandum and Interview February 5, 1954: According to Walter Wyatt, an attorney for the Federal Reserve, it was "the work of career men" in the Federal Reserve that wrote the bill. Joseph P. Dreibelbis said that Wyatt used "paste and a pair of scissors" to draft the bill using past "legislative ideas" as the foundation of the bill.

1933

declare a *"national emergency"*, and close the banks. Section 2 of the bill amended the Trading with the Enemy Act of 1917. Here, too, the bill legalized Roosevelt's prior actions, and justified in law the taking of the people's gold. Section 3 contained the teeth of the bill. This section gave authorization to the Secretary of the Treasury at his discretion to:

"require any or all individuals, partnerships, associations, and corporations to pay and deliver to the Treasurer of the United States any or all gold coin, gold bullion, and gold certificates ... Upon receipt ... the Secretary of the Treasury shall pay therefore an equivalent amount of any other form of coin or currency coined or issued under the laws of the United States ... failing to comply ... shall be subject to a penalty equal to twice the value of the gold or gold certificates ..."

In other words, the Secretary of the Treasury was empowered by law to seize the American people's gold. Although there was no edict to turn over the gold at that point in time there was little doubt the order would come sooner or later.

Adding teeth to the law, violations were subject to a potential $10,000 fine and up to ten years in jail. Each day of the violation was considered a *"separate offense."* In plain language this meant if you crossed paths with the new monetary deists you could be locked up, and the key thrown away.[18]

---

[17] For an excellent synopsis of the legal issues surrounding passage of the bill read "Who Killed the Constitution?" written by Thomas E. Woods, Jr. and Kevin R.C. Gutzman. Pages 83-101.

[18] There were very few prosecutions under the new bill mainly because almost everybody complied with the law. Another reason was the chance

1933

Proclamation 2040: Extending the Emergency

That same day, March 9, 1933, after the Emergency Banking Relief Bill was passed, Roosevelt decreed in Proclamation 2040 that the national emergency would continue indefinitely. For all intents and purposes 2040 had the effect of locking up the gold in the bank vaults. The next day, March 10, 1933, Roosevelt issued Executive Order 6073[19] outlawing the export of gold, gold bullion and gold certificates. In addition, the banks were ordered open again.

Roosevelt Seizes the People's Gold

On April 5, 1933 the moment of truth arrived. It came through Executive Order 6102. This decree by Roosevelt closed the loop on the Emergency Banking Relief Act. Executive Order 6102 ordered the American people to turn in their gold, gold bullion and gold certificates to the Federal Reserve by May 1, 1933. Failure to comply meant a potential $10,000 fine and/or 10 years in jail.

Keen observers noted the divergence between the language of the Executive Order and the fine print of the Banking Relief bill. It was Roosevelt ordering the gold be turned in, and not the Secretary of the Treasury as stipulated in the Banking Relief bill. It didn't matter. Few knew the details of the bill. There was no internet or television. People got information through newspapers, radio and word of mouth. Almost in whole the people did as ordered and turned in their gold. They did so not because they were sheep, but

---

the law would be repealed once the "national emergency" and depression ended.
[19] See Appendix..

rather because they trusted their leaders; they believed that what their leaders were doing was best for the country.

Many thought the gold measures were temporary. And who could fault their optimism? Roosevelt's first Secretary of the Treasury, William Woodin went out of his way to ease the people's concern stating that the move did not mean the United States *"was going off the gold standard."* The move was *"temporary"* according to Roosevelt himself. Indeed, *"it was ridiculous and misleading to say that we have gone off the gold standard,"* Woodin advised the press.[20]

Those in the Roosevelt Administration who objected to leaving the gold standard were hopeful, too, that the moves were one-off events that would be supplanted with future legislation once the banking crisis abated.

Still, it was disheartening to many hard money advocates. The Roosevelt administration obviously was planning to inflate, devalue the currency, ramp up domestic spending and print money to fund spending. The administration belabored its desire to balance the budget. But given the poor state of the economy and the spending measures under consideration there clearly was not enough money that could be raised through taxes to balance the budget.

Those at the time who paid attention to such matters might have remembered Roosevelt's platform during the campaign. What he was doing was the exact opposite of

---

[20] Amity Shlaes, The Forgotten Man: A New History of the Great Depression (New York, NY: HarperCollins Publishers, 2007), 157 Paperback Edition.

what he said he would do if elected. *"We advocate an immediate and drastic reduction of governmental expenditures"* the platform had announced; and a *"sound currency"* coupled with a balanced budget. The reality was striking, although it would take a while for events to unfold.

Yet the die was cast. At this point there was little the average American could do to protect their purchasing power, short of buying silver and/or speculating in mining stocks. It now was illegal for the American people to own gold in the United States. It also was illegal for Americans to own gold outside the United States. Nor could they expect to get their gold back if they read the fine print of Executive Order 6260 issued August 28, 1933. E.O. 6260 stated that the people *did not "retain any interest, legal or equitable" in their gold, gold bullion or gold certificates* once they had turned it in. This meant the people would never see their gold again.

All things considered, the drama surrounding the Emergency Banking Relief Act was the peak of the depression, although pain and suffering would linger for almost another decade. Whether the solutions worked or not is another topic for discussion. Inflation, devaluation and public works projects were chosen to defeat the economic and banking disasters of the day. A return to sound money and the domestic gold standard was not in the cards.

1933

Dollar Devaluation

Whenever the legislators endeavor to take away and destroy the property of the people, or to reduce them to slavery under arbitrary power, they put themselves into a state of war with the people, who are thereupon absolved from any farther obedience, and are left to the common refuge which God hath provided for all men against force and violence. **John Locke**.

Nine months after the seizure of the people's gold the Congress on January 30, 1934 passed, and Roosevelt signed into law, the Gold Reserve Act. The *"traitorous hoarders"* of gold thus were proven exactly correct in their assessment of the government's future course of action regarding dollar devaluation. In the Gold Reserve Act the dollar was devalued from $20.67 per gold ounce to $35 per gold ounce, a nearly 70 percent devaluation. There was no scientific or economic reason why $35 per ounce was chosen. Paraphrasing the words of his advisors, $35 was just a number that Roosevelt seemed to fancy.

The chronicles of the day are quite amusing. In his bed early in the morning the President would meet with his financial team. They would discuss the latest events and then the talk would turn to the price of gold. While still in his pajamas Roosevelt would fix the price. What the Bank of England, the Federal Reserve or the free market thought mattered not. It was Roosevelt and Roosevelt alone that determined the price of gold.

"One day he would move the price up several cents; another, a few more. One morning, FDR told his group he was thinking of raising the gold price by twenty-one cents.

1933

Why that figure, his entourage asked? It's a lucky number, Roosevelt said, because it's three times seven." Later, Henry Morgenthau, Jr., the Secretary of the Treasury, wrote that *"If anybody knew how we really set the gold price through a combination of lucky numbers, etc., I think they would be frightened."*[21]

Many Americans, naturally, were bitter at the brazen theft of their property. The government paid the people $20.67 for each ounce of gold they turned in. And less than a year later the price was $35 per ounce. The government, of course, pocketed the difference. Yet, as noted, this was an age where most Americans trusted their leaders. The age of transparency, instant communication and the internet was decades in the future. Trusting their leaders, the American people tendered their gold to the government thinking, hoping, praying that it would be a temporary situation, and that eventually they would get their gold back.

Close observers might have disabused the hopeful people of this notion, reminding them of the *"hoarding"* and *"unpatriotic"* rhetoric coming from Roosevelt. In addition, the people might have benefitted from remembering Roosevelt had blamed the banking crisis on the very people who had redeemed their money for gold. In any event, the masses learned soon enough as the days passed in the first year of the Roosevelt administration that they had seen the last of their gold.

This brash act by Roosevelt and Congress is the very reason the framers had written into the Constitution a hard money doctrine. The framers had experienced firsthand the

---

[21] Shlaes, The Forgotten Man: A New History of the Great Depression, 147-8. Paperback Edition.

1933

devastation of inflation during the Revolution with the Continental. The framers clearly wanted to limit the government's capacity to inflate and devalue the people's currency with printed paper money. That was the reason why the framers defined the dollar as 371 ¼ grains silver. A silver dollar once and forever minted with 371 ¼ grains of silver by definition cannot be devalued.

But the deal was done. The people's gold had been seized. The dollar had been devalued. Roosevelt now was free to spend, inflate and *"experiment"* on the domestic front without fear of the people redeeming their devalued dollars for gold.

Key Legislative Events of 1933/4[22]

Proclamation 2038 called Congress into extra session on March 9, 1933.

Proclamation 2039 declared a "national emergency" and a national banking holiday from March 6, 1933 to March 9, 1933. Bank disbursements by of silver, gold and currency were banned during the period.

The Emergency Banking Relief Act passed on March 9, 1933 by the Congress sanctioned the Secretary of the Treasury at his discretion to require the American people to turn over *"to the Treasurer of the United States any or all gold coin, gold bullion, and gold certificates"* for payment by *"an equivalent amount of any another United States coin*

---

[22] Michael S. Rozeff, *The U.S. Constitution and Money: Corruption and Decline. The Writer's Free Internet Edition* – Volume III. (East Amherst, 2010). Also see Rozeff, Michael. S. *The U.S. Constitution and Money*, Part 9, The Gold Seizure: Presidential and Legislative Action for an excellent summary on this section.

or currency coined or issued under the laws of the United States ..."

Executive Order 6073 issued on March 10, 1933 ordered that gold may not be exported out of the United States or transferred from any bank. All movement of gold was halted by this order.

Executive Order 6102 issued on April 5, 1933 by Roosevelt, rather than the Secretary of the Treasury as mandated in the Emergency Banking Relief Act, required the American people *"to deliver on or before May 1, 1933, to a Federal Reserve Bank or a branch or agency thereof or to any member bank of the Federal Reserve System all gold coin, gold bullion and gold certificates ..."* Restitution would come through payment by *"an equivalent amount of any other form of coin or currency coined or issued under the laws of the United States ..."*

Congress made Federal Reserve Notes and National Bank Notes into legal tender in the Agricultural Adjustment Act on May 12, 1933. The President at his discretion also was authorized to devalue the gold dollar *"as he finds necessary from his investigation to stabilize domestic prices or to protect the foreign commerce against the adverse effect of depreciated foreign currencies ..."*

Gold clauses were banned in contracts on June 5, 1933 through House Resolution 192. This resolution was passed with the understanding that since the American people could not possess gold then the clauses in contracts stipulating payment in gold were de facto null and void, too.

On June 16, 1933, FDR signed into law the Banking Act of 1933 which created the Federal Deposit Insurance

Corporation. Through this legislation banking deposits were backed by tax payer dollars. Tax payer backing of bank deposits in this legislation is credited with stopping the widespread banking closures of the 1930's.

Executive Order 6260 issued on August 28, 1933 by Roosevelt, rather than the Secretary of the Treasury as mandated in the Emergency Banking Relief Act, limited gold from being acquired and/or held (hoarded) by all except a Federal Reserve Bank. Section 11 of the order stated: *"The Executive Orders of April 5, 1933, Forbidding the Hoarding of Gold Coin, Gold Bullion and Gold Certificates, and April 20, 1933, relating to Foreign Exchange and the Earmarking and Export of Gold Coin or Bullion or Currency, respectively, are hereby revoked."*

The purpose of E.O. 6260 was to tidy up legal loose ends. But it fell short. The order for the American people to turn over their gold yet again came from Roosevelt and not the Secretary of the Treasury as required in the Emergency Banking Relief Act. By this point it didn't really matter. Most of the people in the United States, unaware of the fine print, already had delivered their gold to the banks. Importantly, E.O. 6260 stated that the people did not *"retain any interest, legal or equitable"* in their gold, gold bullion or gold certificates once they had turned it over to the government, meaning they would never see it again.

On December 28, 1933 the error of E.O. 6260 was corrected. Acting Secretary of the Treasury, Henry Morgenthau, Jr. issued an order *"requiring the delivery of gold coin, gold bullion, and gold certificates to the Treasurer of the United States ..."* This order rectified the mistakes in the April 5 and August 28 executive orders issued by

1933

Roosevelt. The purpose of this order was to make official the requirement in the Emergency Banking Relief Act that the Secretary of the Treasury order the gold delivered to the Federal Reserve Banks, who would act as guardians of the gold.

The final insult to the American people was delivered on January 30, 1934. The Gold Reserve Act was passed in Congress. This act revalued gold from $20.67 to $35, a roughly seventy percent devaluation of the dollar against gold. The act also consigned all the gold delivered by the American people to the Federal Reserve Banks to the United States Treasury. The Federal Reserve Banks were given gold certificates representing the actual gold. Eventually the gold seized from the people was stored at Fort Knox once the facility was built.

Summary

In 1933 FDR rammed through Congress legislative acts that seized the people's gold, outlawed gold clauses in contracts, devalued the dollar and backstopped bank deposits with taxpayer money.

The year 1933 was a dark year for supporters of honest, constitutional money. Under dubious legal remedies the American people were forced under threat of fines and jail time to turn over their privately held, constitutionally legal gold holdings to the government. By this action gold coins were removed from circulation. The people were paid for this injustice by and large with paper money which was subsequently devalued from $20.67 per gold ounce to $35 per gold ounce. In addition, payment in gold on its commitments such as those payable to holders of U.S. bonds was stopped, or more accurately, defaulted. Adding insult to injury, gold clauses in contracts were outlawed which stood to protect creditors from government deprivations such as the 1933 dollar devaluation.

The end result of this travesty was as predictable as it was certain. Without the discipline of gold, the Federal Reserve has printed paper money in ever increasing amounts. So much paper money has been printed that the once gold backed dollar has lost over 95% of its 1933 purchasing power. This is why the cost of goods and services continue to rise in the United States.

Excessive printing of paper money dollars is a perfect example of supply and demand economics. The more paper dollars printed the less the value. Put another way, it took $20.67 to buy one ounce of gold in 1933. In 2012 it takes roughly $1800 to buy the same ounce of gold. This is the very reason the framers instituted a definition of the dollar in terms of silver and gold. The framers through their own personal experiences knew that if paper money, unchecked by silver and gold, ever gained a foothold again in America it would be devalued and inflated until it was worthless. It happened during the paper money experiment in the early American colonies with the Continental, and it's happening again today.

FDR's 1933 Gold Legislative Initiatives

Betrayed the Constitution. Betrayed the People.

Chapter 7

Bretton Woods and the Nixon Shock

Predestined to Fail

Toward the end of World War II, the allied powers met in Bretton Woods, New Hampshire to draw up a post-war monetary system. At the time all the great powers were on a paper money system as they had been in World War I. The year was 1944. Named for the town in which they met, the Bretton Woods agreement fashioned an international basis for currency exchange.

The great powers in effort to promote free trade and pay postwar reconstruction fixed their exchange rates to the United States dollar. To add teeth and stability to the plan the representatives of the various nations agreed to keep their currencies within a one percent fixed rate band versus the dollar. Each country would manage their target by buying and selling dollars in the foreign exchange markets to maintain parity. The United States did its part by tying the dollar to gold at $35 per ounce. Foreigners, though not U.S. citizens, could redeem dollars for gold at $35 per ounce.[1] The dollar, at least for foreigners, thus was made to appear as good as gold.

---

[1] The conversion right included foreign citizens as well as foreign governments. After 1962 the right of conversion of dollars to gold was limited to foreign governments.

Basically, the goal of the Bretton Woods system was to create exchange rate stability between nations without using gold as the backdrop for currencies except the dollar. In practice the Bretton Woods agreement did the exact opposite, or as Henry Hazlitt wrote: *"The specific provisions ... not only permitted but encouraged internal inflation, devaluation and exchange instability."*[2] John Maynard Keynes, the author of much of the Bretton Woods agreement, called the monetary scheme of the agreement the *"exact opposite"* of the gold standard.[3]

The fundamental success of the program depended on the prudent exercise of fiscal and trade practices of the United States authorities. The stability of the dollar also was crucial. Yet the dollar was not a stable currency given the huge deficits and accumulating debt the United States had amassed while prosecuting World War II. This placed the entirety of the Bretton Woods system in the hands of politicians and the like rather than the free market. Given the burgeoning increase in the size and scope of government in the United States this had all the earmarks of failure written on it.

Included in the Bretton Woods agreements was the creation of the International Monetary fund and a currency stabilization fund. An interesting proviso in the agreement was that the stabilization fund *"would be forced to buy depreciated currencies far above their market values, regardless of the reasons for the depreciation."* In fact, the

---

[2] Henry Hazlitt, From Bretton Woods to World Inflation: A Study of Causes and Consequences (Chicago, Illinois: Regnery Gateway, 2009), p. 60

[3] Hazlitt, From Bretton Woods to World Inflation: A Study of Causes and Consequences, p. 115.

agreement encouraged currency devaluation albeit on a *"uniform proportionate"* basis *"to make resort to inflation easy smooth, and above all respectable."* The signers knew the seeds of inflation lay embedded in the agreement of course. They planned to overcome the natural skew of inflation by controlling the price of commodities. In other words, the powers planned state control over the world economy rather than allowing free market principles to sort things out.[4]

About the time that the Bretton Woods agreement was signed the United States had roughly 25,000 tons of gold. Throughout the 1950's the Bretton Woods system worked reasonably well. Admittedly, the United States authorities spent, printed and inflated the volume of dollars. But such was the state of destruction in the world after World War II that many of the countries liberated by the United States chose not to incite their liberator and benefactor by excessive dollar to gold exchanges.

As time passed it became clear the United States authorities had not and would not curb domestic spending; nor would the United States authorities exercise restraint on printing the world's main currency. Looking over the horizon it was clear that eventually the price of gold would breach the $35 per ounce conversion level even though throughout the 1950's the level had held. The case was quite evident. The price of gold wanted to go up, or more accurately, the price of the dollar wanted to drop against gold. This was evident given that the gold reserves of the

---

[4] Hazlitt, From Bretton Woods to World Inflation: A Study of Causes and Consequences, p. 126.

United States were tumbling. The market was shouting loudly that it did not like the increasing trade and budget deficits which the United States was running.

The London Gold Pool

Presently after President Kennedy was inaugurated in January 1961 Treasury officials recommended that the United States and Europe syndicate their gold assets. The goal was to stop market forces from running the price of gold above the authorized rate of $35 per ounce. This led to the creation of the London Gold Pool in 1961 whose mission was to suppress the price of gold, and preserve the Bretton Woods system as long as possible. Taking action on this proposal the central banks of the United States, Britain, West Germany, France, Switzerland, Italy, Belgium, Netherlands, and Luxembourg established the London Gold Pool in the early months of 1961.

To stop the rise of gold the United States and the central banks of Europe sold massive amounts of gold through the good offices of the pool to suppress the price. For a while the London Gold Pool held its own. Yet it was doomed to fail from the beginning. The market absorbed the gold selling and then some. Meanwhile, the gold reserves of the United States steadily dropped as emboldened foreigners converted to gold their overvalued dollars. By the mid 1960's, with the war on poverty, the Cold War and the Vietnam War in full swing, the breaking point almost had arrived. Fiscal deficits, accumulating debt and trade deficits of the United States could no longer be ignored.

The catalyst arrived when Britain devalued the pound in late 1967. This led to an enormous move upward in the price of gold. In March of 1968 the United States and the central banks of Europe admitted defeat and closed down the price suppression techniques and market manipulation of the London Gold Pool. By this time the gold reserves of the United States had dropped to roughly 10,000 tons, a drop of about 60% from the peak.

Silver Certificate Default

About the same time the London Gold Pool closed shop the United States defaulted on its silver obligations. This travesty happened on June 24th, 1968 when the United States government ended the right of the people to redeem silver certificates for physical bullion. Silver certificates had circulated widely within the economy in the aftermath of FDR's actions in 1933. Mainly silver certificates circulated in small denominations, usually $1 bills. On the face of the dollar bill was the famous clause stating: *"One Dollar in Silver Payable to the Bearer on Demand."*

As with gold the price of silver was pushing ever higher in the market. People had the option of spending their silver certificates; or they could present their silver certificates to the Treasury and receive silver bullion. For example, with silver trading less than $1 per ounce silver certificate holders had no incentive to redeem their certificates since they would receive back less than $1 in silver bullion. But above $1 per ounce the holder had all the incentive in the world to redeem the certificate since he would receive back more than $1 in bullion.

As government deficits started to pile up, the price of silver, in lockstep with gold, moved steadily higher. By the middle of 1961 the price was flirting with $1 per ounce after spending the decade of the 1950's below $1. By late 1962 the price was approaching $1.30 per ounce. The public took advantage of the price discrepancy and took the bullion, exactly as the previous generation had done with their redeemable gold dollars. Redemption of silver certificates continued apace through the mid 1960's, and then went into overdrive as silver screamed higher. The high was $2.57 in 1968. It was at this point that the right to redeem ended.

Coincident with the redemption of silver certificates the public began to pull silver coins out of circulation. As with the certificates, the silver content in the coinage was greater than the face amount of the coin. To counter the discrepancy the government reduced the silver content in the coinage to reflect the new reality, just as the Romans and Greeks had done two thousand years earlier. Eventually, all silver content would be eliminated in the U.S. coins exactly as had been the case with the Romans and Greeks.

Thus, for the second time in the 20th Century the United States government reneged on a covenant with the people. Since 1933 the people had been forbidden to own gold. As a consolation, silver had provided the potential for protection against paper money devaluation. During the price controls of the 1940's the people had not worried too much about inflation. The result was that silver dropped to a 45:1 ratio against gold. You might remember that at the time of the Coinage Act in 1792 the ratio had been set at 15:1.

Once price controls were lifted in the late 1940's the prices of goods and services zoomed higher. It took a while but eventually the market price of silver began to reflect reality. Once it did, the government almost immediately broke the covenant. Just as the Romans, rather than admit that it was their very own policies that were causing the price of silver to reflect the reality of money printing the government simply changed the rules during the middle of the game, and reneged.

After Britain's devaluation, the failure of the London Gold Pool and the American silver default the leading signatory nations of the Bretton Woods agreement saw the writing on the wall. The dollar obviously was over-valued as had been the pound. Indeed, maintaining their currencies within the fixed one percent band versus the dollar had become too difficult. Simply stated, the cost of buying and selling currency in the foreign exchange market to maintain the fixed rates was too expensive.

The market literally was shouting for change, namely, a devaluation of the dollar. Thus in 1971 Germany, Holland, Austria, Belgium and Switzerland took action. The whole Bretton Woods system began to unravel when these countries stopped their currency manipulations. Without government intervention a free market in currency trading emerged. Price discovery was the immediate consequence. Broad movements higher resulted for these currencies against the dollar. Given the scope of the problem this was the least bad solution for the people of the United States. As it happened, so many dollar claims in gold were outstanding that if all the claims were exchanged the people's gold in the United States Treasury would have been emptied several fold over.

The free float of the key European currencies and the de-facto devaluation of the dollar changed the game for the United States. While the actual flow of gold from the United States had been relatively small the first few months of 1971, the outflow picked up speed materially as the months wore on. Currency speculators naturally piled on as the news increasingly deteriorated on the fiscal and trade fronts in the United States. As the news worsened the flow of gold out of the United States forced a reaction.

National Bankruptcy

On August 15, 1971 President Nixon in a televised broadcast declared that the United States no longer would honor its international commitment to exchange gold for dollars. This effectively put the Bretton Woods system out of its misery. At that moment in time, the monetary system of the United States, and the rest of the world for that matter, morphed into a paper money, free floating currency system, with no gold backing. Paper money thus once again was left to the avarices and good offices of government authorities as in the days of the Continental.

The abrupt action by Nixon was an admission that the United States was bankrupt. The fact of the matter was that the United States could no longer live up to its promise under the Bretton Woods Agreement to convert dollars to gold. There were simply too many dollars floating around the world begging to be converted to gold. And as her leaders publically and privately admitted, the United States did not have enough gold to meet the demand.

It was obvious the leadership of the United States, past and present, had not been good stewards of the world's reserve currency. Foreigners, so to speak, were voting with their check books. They knew the dollar was overvalued. They knew the United States would not stop spending and running budget and trade deficits. Commitments made by the

United States were too big. Foreigners wanted to unload their dollar reserves and get gold while there was still some gold available in U.S. vaults before a big devaluation slapped them in the face. But the Unites States preempted them, and placed the blame on currency "speculators."

The Smithsonian Agreement

Huge moves against the dollar ensued over the next few months. In the meantime the United States and their reluctant trade partners tried to outmaneuver the market with a head fake. In December of 1971 the Smithsonian Agreement was announced. This was an effort to put the genie back in the bottle.

The Smithsonian Agreement revalued downward the dollar against other currencies as had existed under the Bretton Woods arrangement. The fixed price of gold was valued upward from $35 to $38.02 although it mattered little because under the new fixed ratios of the major currencies gold was not redeemable. Regardless, even $38.02 was unrealistic. The free market price of gold was considerably higher, and would go even higher. In 1972 the price of gold ranged from $44 to $69.30. For 1973 the price ranged from $63.90 to $127. And on and on it went until in 1980 the price of gold reached $850 per ounce.

Yet the Smithsonian machination was but a temporary stopgap measure even as it was described as the *"greatest monetary agreement in the history of the world"* by President Nixon. Be that as it may, the Smithsonian Agreement lasted for fourteen months before it too crashed and burned. In vain the various nations attempted to keep the dollar in alignment. But the forces of nature were too strong.

There wasn't enough money or political capital in the capitols of America's trading partners to maintain the price of the over-valued dollar given her fiscal and trade imbalances.

Since 1971 little has changed. In essence, all the major currencies of the world trade relative to each other and not gold. A short while after the closing of the gold window by President Nixon, rules were erected by the International Monetary Fund prohibiting currency prices to reference gold in valuation. No longer did The United States have to concern itself with her trading partners exchanging dollars for gold. Nor does the United States, or any other country for that matter, have to worry about inflation, trade deficits or budget deficits affecting its gold ownership.

Each country of the world now is in control of its currency. The result has been inflation and devaluation of the weaker currencies against the prudent. Yet devaluation is precisely what some interested stakeholder's want, namely exporters, who with a devalued currency hold a distinct competitive advantage against their competitors in countries with prudent currency managers.

This has now gone on for over 40 years. During this time, without the discipline of the gold standard on government officials, budget deficits, trade deficits, debt, money printing and inflation have risen to astronomical levels.

This is a crushing situation for the people who do not receive the first fruits of an inflationary policy. The end result has been exactly as predicted by Austrian school economists who knew from history exactly what would happen once the binds of gold were loosened from policy makers. What needs to be done to correct this situation will be discussed in Chapter 8.

Summary

The Bretton Woods Agreement was a phony gold exchange system relying on the fiscal prudence of American legislators. The dollar became the key reserve currency of the world. The United States agreed to exchange dollars for gold at $35 per ounce. Given the fiscal impulsiveness of American lawmakers the agreement stood no chance of success.

The Bretton Woods Agreement was established in 1944 between the major western powers of the world. Many of the signatories of the agreement came from countries whose economies and infrastructure had been severely hampered if not devastated during World War II. At the time the U.S. had the strongest economy and was the engine of growth for the world, at least in terms of fueling the essential rebuilding program. Because of this the U.S. was hands down the strongest pillar of the group. For her money and leadership the dollar was established as the reserve currency of the world, an enormously prestigious and powerful national policy tool.

The purpose of the Bretton Woods meeting and agreement was to make preparations to rebuild the world economy after World War II. A system of rules, protocols and institutions such as the International Monetary Fund and the International Bank for Reconstruction and Development were established. A system of fixed exchange rates was created. Each country agreed to manage its currency's parity with the dollar within a one percent band. As a token to her determination to exercise good stewardship of the dollar the United States agreed to exchange dollars for gold on demand.

Bretton Woods was doomed to fail from the beginning. The budget and trade deficits of the United States made her trade partners nervous. Given the right to convert dollars foreign nations increasingly exchanged their accumulated dollars for gold through the 1950's, 60's and 70's. Despite widespread efforts to stop the exchange of dollars for gold the loss of gold eventually became intolerable and President Nixon closed the gold window in 1971 thus ending the Bretton Woods Agreement. The Smithsonian Agreement was a last gasp effort to maintain international currency parity. It too was doomed to fail, and it did with fourteen months. With the ending of the Smithsonian all currency pairing efforts ceased. Currencies to this day trade against each other. There is no gold or silver link.

Bretton Woods Agreement

Phony Gold Standard. Doomed to Fail.

Chapter 8

Concluding Remarks

The Constitutional Dollar is Dead: What Can You Do?

There is a tide in the affairs of men,
Which, taken at the flood, leads on to fortune;
Omitted, all the voyage of their life
Is bound in shallows and in miseries.
On such a full sea are we now afloat;
And we must take the current when it serves,
Or lose our ventures.

Brutus
The Life and Death of Julius Caesar
Shakespeare

    The constitutional dollar as defined by the framers is dead. That much is patently obvious. The history outlined in *Dollar Default* has shown clearly how the action steps taken by the heirs of our republic have severed any connection to the original meaning of the dollar as defined by the framers.

    The dollar was determined by the free market to be the medium of exchange in the American colonies. It was adopted from Spain long before the revolution. And what was the dollar? The dollar was a Spanish milled coin of silver. Because of her significant commercial and international position at the time, Spanish milled coins of various denominations circulated widely throughout the colonies. They were known for their accurate weights,

Concluding Remarks

measures and general trustworthiness. The market spoke and adopted these coins as the leading medium of exchange. By 1704 the usage of the Spanish silver dollar was so widespread that Queen Anne of England made it official. The queen issued a proclamation decreeing that foreign coin in the American colonies were to be regulated according to the "weight and fineness" of the Spanish silver coins, the predominant coin of the colonies.

After the revolution the framers got down to brass tacks. Given that the free market had adopted the Spanish milled silver coin as the nation's medium of exchange an appropriate definition of its weight and measures had to be established. Thus, before meeting at the Constitutional Convention in 1787 Thomas Jefferson voiced:

"If we determine that a dollar shall be our unit, we must then say with precision what a dollar is. This coin as struck at different times, of different weight and fineness, is of different values."

The framers agreed and took decisive action. This was accomplished first by authorizing in the Constitution that Congress was the sole authority in coining money through a standard of weights and measures; and second through passage of the Coinage Act of 1792 which defined the dollar in terms of silver, namely, 371 4/16 grains silver, which itself was defined in terms of gold.

All of this changed when Congress turned over its constitutional authority to coin money in 1913 to a third party entity, the Federal Reserve. As matters have devolved since 1913 the dollar is not measured or defined in terms of silver, much less gold, as the framers wrote into law.

Concluding Remarks

Without a definition or measurement, one is left to wonder exactly what a dollar is. It's certainly not a weight or measure of silver. And it certainly is not a weight or measure of gold. The best I can fathom is that a dollar is a piece of paper with green ink on it stating: "this note is legal tender for all debts, public and private." In other words, a dollar is whatever the Federal Reserve or the Congress says it is.

What can we do about this pitiful state of affairs? On the legislative front, not much I'm afraid. The vested interests have captured Congress lock, stock and barrel.

But I can tell you with certainty when things will change.

Change will come when the pain of change is less than the pain of staying the same.

The free market will do the job. You will be amazed how fast the constitutional dollar returns. At the end of the grand experiment of paper money the people will become so fed up with the status quo that a veritable free market revolution will overwhelm the vested political and business interests. At some point the devaluation of the dollar, government debt, deficits and the rising cost of living will become so unbearable that the American people, her leaders, the business community and our international trade partners will rise as one and say – no more.

Typically, a paper money system lasts about forty years. Our grand experiment started in 1971. So we're at the average duration in 2012. If one listens closely there's no shortage of grumbling. The pressure in the cauldron is building.

Concluding Remarks

The Answer to Three Questions

In the Preface I posed three questions that *Dollar Default* intended to answer. 1) Why did the heirs to sound constitutional money reinstitute paper money which was the exact opposite of what the framers created? 2) Who were the beneficiaries of this revolutionary change? 3) Who pays for the change?

Hopefully, if you've stuck with me this far, you'll know the answers without my stating the obvious.

First, the bankers that created the Federal Reserve in 1913 wanted a partner armed with the ability to inflate and create money from nothing. That's what the bankers meant when they said they needed an elastic currency. The gold standard foiled the banker's goals of low risk, perpetual, easy profits. It made life too hard for them to make money. From the beginning the banks wanted the Fed at beck and call to backstop bad loans and panics. Ultimately, the goal was the creation of a cartel that protected the bankers from free market competition with sizeable barriers to entry.

Second, the main beneficiary of paper money obviously is the banking world. Bank deposits are backed by the tax payer. This allows bankers to lend depositor money with impunity. Bankers know that if loans go bad the taxpayer will pick up the tab with no adverse financial penalty on the banker. In the meantime, the banks rack up profits, and pay out bonuses to the bankers. Government benefits immensely, too. With the Fed at its side government has the ability to grow to unimaginable levels. The Fed simply buys government bonds through open market operations, and monetizes the debt. Thus, the government can create and fund whatever program it wants. Don't believe me? Simply observe the growth of government from 1792 until 1913. Then look at government growth since the creation of the Fed. With the gold standard the government has to exercise fiscal prudence. Without it there is no mechanism to control spending.

The answer to the third question is that the average man in the street pays for the luxury of the banks and the Fed. They pay through the nose in terms of higher prices as more and more money is printed. They pay through a devalued currency. Yet the average guy does not benefit from the new arrangement. Recessions are not shorter. Nor are expansions noticeably longer because of Fed *"scientific management."* In other words, the average guy gets none of the benefits. But he bears all the downside.

A First Step Back to Constitutional Money

As matters exist today the paper money in your wallet, Federal Reserve Notes, is money in the United States economy. My view is that we need to return to a free market based monetary system like that which existed at the time the Constitution and Coinage Act were drafted into law. The easiest way to make this transition is to institute redemption claims of Federal Reserve Notes for gold and silver. In other words, Federal Reserve Notes would be the same thing as gold or silver coins. Backing the notes would be 100% gold and silver - no half-way measures allowed.

Detractors say there would not be enough gold and silver to institute such a policy. This may be true if gold is priced at $42.22 as it is currently on the Treasury's balance sheet. But gold is worth a lot more in the free market.

Concluding Remarks

The path to making Federal Reserve Notes backed 100% by gold is *price*.

Here's how it would work. The United States Treasury has 258,641,851 fine troy ounces of gold on its books.[1] The monetary base in the United States, M1, which accounts for cash in circulation, coins, checking accounts and savings accounts, comes to about $2.252 trillion.[2] Dividing M1 by the total amount of ounces of gold calculates to $8707.

Thus, the price of gold at $8707 would cover the monetary base of the United States 100% by gold. This means that every Federal Reserve Note in your wallet would be backed 100% by gold. So if you chose, you could convert your cash to gold exactly as the framers intended. With gold backing 100% of the money supply the United States would take a huge step back toward constitutional principles.

I realize more thought and work needs to be put into such a plan. What I'm pointing out is that a return to Constitutional money is possible. It is the *price* of gold that is the key first step to making the move feasible. Actually, we're closer to this happening than one might think.

Consider the fact that, as far as we know, the amount of gold in the Treasury has stayed the same since 1971. As noted this amount is 258,641,851 ounces. The dollar amount of Treasury gold at current market prices using $1800 per ounce comes to $465,555,331,800, or 20.67% of the money supply. Balance this with the fact that in 1933 at the time FDR confiscated the people's gold the required gold reserve

---

[1] April 30, 2012 Gold Status Report of the U.S. Treasury.
[2] Numbers from the St. Louis Federal Reserve for May 11, 2012.

ratio for banks was 40%. So, in actual fact, the United States is not too far removed from the metrics of the gold standard which existed in 1933, pre-confiscation.

Again, *price* is the key element to instituting the gold standard.

The second step in return to Constitutional money is to reel in the Federal Reserve. It needs to be closed as soon as possible. The Federal Reserve is little more than a special interest group programmed to serve its own interests through jobs, influence and power. Like any bureaucracy, once formed, its sole mission becomes one of survival.

Lest you think that I'm being presumptuous to recommend eliminating the Federal Reserve, even if you accept the failures of the Fed listed in Chapter 5, consider the following:

"It is one of the serious evils of our present system of banking that it enables one class of society - and that by no means a numerous one - by its control over the currency, to act injuriously upon the interests of all the others and to exercise more than its just proportion of influence in political affairs."

Andrew Jackson, *Farewell Address March 4, 1837*

So as you can see, the struggle against entrenched banking power in the United States is nothing new. The framers fought over central banking, the Jefferson administration fought over it, the Madison administration fought over it and so did the Jackson Administration. Fast forward to modern times and we're still fighting over central

Concluding Remarks

banking. The only difference between then and now is the name of the institution: the Federal Reserve.

As noted in Chapter 5 the Fed states that one of its missions is to maintain permanent nominal demand growth to attain full employment. This is a gallant goal but there's always another side to the story. Maintaining permanent demand growth requires permanent credit growth, which necessitates permanent debt growth which ultimately leads to public enslavement to bankers. At the end of the day the bankers, and their surrogate the Federal Reserve, will decide that inflation becomes a commercial imperative if not national security goal in effort to ease the encumbrance of paying back debt.

Federal Reserve bankers and officials would like you to believe that what they do is very difficult, requiring years of education, training and study. This is nonsense. They have a computer. It's easy for Federal Reserve accountants to type a few numbers into an excel spreadsheet under a column labeled "deposits" at the bank. The Fed calls these computer entries "money." At this point the Fed writes a check, wires the "money" or journals it to a government bond dealer such as J.P. Morgan or Citibank. In exchange for the "money" the Fed receives government bonds from the dealer who bought the bonds originally from the Treasury at auction. The Fed then collects the interest on the bond. Sometimes the Fed will hold the bonds for a long time. Other times they'll sell the bond to another party. These are called open market operations. That's how it's done. It's not hard at all to understand or implement. Just remember that the whole process started with the Fed creating money out of nothing. By the way, if you do this, you go to jail.

Concluding Remarks

There's more to the process naturally.[3] Yet none of these processes are difficult. Of course, the Fed would like you to believe that only a Ph.D. can do it. This is laughable.

At the same time, it's as easy as can be for the Federal Reserve to hot shot paper money to banks for customers who prefer cash. It costs roughly two cents to print a $1 dollar Federal Reserve Note. The Fed essentially sprinkles green ink on paper, calls it legal tender for all debts public and private and sends it to the banks as money. This is the exact same thing that took place during the revolution with the Continental. The only difference is that a small team of Treasury officials did it during the revolution rather than the sprawling, bureaucratic Fed.

As you can imagine, there are powerful vested interests resisting a return to Constitutional money. Have no illusions, dear reader. The vested interests will fight tooth and nail to maintain their position of power in the current arrangement. The fact is that the vested interest – bankers, government bureaucrats, welfare recipients and government contractors, the military machine, etc. – love paper money. These groups protect the status quo because they directly benefit from the paper money scam. It is these groups that get access to the first fruits of newly issued digital money or paper money before it devalues.

With gold as the standard monetary unit the key beneficiaries of paper money lose their perch. Under the umbrella of the gold standard, a pure, uncorrupted barrier to inflation prevents the rise of the money supply because of

---

[3] Through open market operations the Fed increases or decreases the money supply by buying or selling government bonds. This mechanism allows the Fed to control, theoretically, the speed the economy grows.

Concluding Remarks

the automatic loss of gold from the offending country. This is why a cacophony of vitriol is poured on gold by Federal Reserve economists, central bankers, treasury officials and financial journalists who are part of the club.

With the gold standard, bad policy is immediately exposed as gold leaves the country. The loss of gold, naturally, would force a change in direction which would disturb politicians eager to buy votes with *"free"* government handouts made possible by the printing of money. Thus, it is easy to gauge why the vested interests despise gold. It's because gold demands restraint, good stewardship and virtue, which is why there is such a concerted effort to disparage gold and silver from the historical record. Yet while central bankers cannot erase from memory the history of silver and gold as money, it just may be that history erases central bankers and their little paper money fiatscos from history.

Before this happens, the fact of the matter is that there is no limit to how large the numbers – *debt* - can grow. And while government debt may seem staggering now, just wait another ten years. If the system stays the same the debt will be larger still, because as long as the Fed enables the government through the creation of money from nothing, and people accept it, then it will continue until people wise up to the fraud. At that point Federal Reserve Notes will be rejected just as was the Continental.

Concluding Remarks

Some Good News

In the meantime, what can you do?

In 1975 Congress passed legislation allowing the American people to once again own physical gold. This legislation gave the people the right to protect themselves from dollar devaluation through direct ownership of gold. Even among central banks there's a positive development of late. Whereas in the past central banks were liquidating their gold holdings now they are buying huge amounts of physical. Central banks from Russia to China to India are loading their vaults once again with gold.

It's almost as if the central banks of the world have started their own version of an automatic investment plan like a 401k. They appear to be buying gold each month on a set schedule if the press reports are to be believed. My sense is that central banks have gotten nervous about the tremendous amount of paper money they themselves have printed. So they have decided to do what people have done for thousands of years. They're protecting themselves by adding to their existing gold stock.

A second possibility exists also why central banks are buying gold. It might be that central banks see the writing on the wall for paper money. It could be that what they are doing is buying as much gold as they can in anticipation of a return to the gold standard, and they want to have a large supply when gold becomes the anchor of currencies once again. After all, there was a changing of the guard in 1787, 1933, 1968 and 1971. Who's to say there won't be another change in 2012?

Concluding Remarks

There is but one feature that protects the dollar from disintegration. That feature is its station as the world reserve currency. If the dollar is replaced as the world reserve currency the benefits of holding it vanishes in the twinkling of an eye. Backed by nothing but colossal and hopelessly un-payable government debt, the dollar sits terrifyingly atop a mountain of dynamite, surrounded by a raging wall of fire, waiting for the flash of detonation.

This is pure speculation, but if the dollar is devalued it might be devalued against a "new" global currency called the SDR. SDR's, short for Special Drawing Rights, would be a basket of currencies controlled by the International Monetary Fund, and used for international trade. On the other hand, if the dollar needs to be replaced after a hyperinflationary event, my hunch is that the new dollar would be the same as the old dollar, but with less zeroes at the end.

A word of caution needs to be said at this point. Don't expect to get rich if you decide to buy gold or silver. You might get rich, but that's a side effect. Think of physical ownership of gold and silver as an insurance contract against disaster. What you're doing is protecting yourself against a total wipeout if the paper dollars in your wallet become worthless a la the Continental. Stated another way, with gold you have your wealth stored in money that maintains purchasing power regardless of what happens. But let's say the dollar does go the way of the Continental. What will happen in all probability is that your gold and silver holdings will be valued at infinity against worthless money in your wallet. So what you gain in gold and silver you lose against cash.

Concluding Remarks

Yet if there is a dollar debacle and you own a mortgage you'll be able to pay it off with what amounts to Monopoly money. This exact scenario happened during the revolution with the Continental. But if you're a landlord you'll be collecting the same Monopoly money until the contract expires, which is why, by the way, contracts back in the day had a gold clause in them for payment in gold – just in case. Our forefathers were wise to the old trick of devaluation because they lived during the destructive period of the Continental. In any event, it's quite possible that you'll wind up spending your gold and silver to buy food or pay for medical services should *that day* ever arrive. Who knows if it is so? But then again, you'll be infinitely better off than the poor souls without gold or silver in their possession.

The same observation needs to be said about your stock portfolio. I have no idea how stocks will react if the dollar implodes. Maybe stocks will drop as investors cash out to buy gold and silver. Or maybe they will rise as they suddenly discount a lower dollar. In Weimar Germany stocks rose sharply after an initial drop when the hyperinflationary event seized the country in the early 1920's. Based on my experience over a thirty year career working with clients many, if not most, will not be able to tolerate a crushing drop in their stock portfolio before a retracement back up, if that's what happens. I saw fear first hand in 1987, 1989, 1997, 1998 and 2001. It's not pretty. Clients basically sold regardless of price, or what might happen on the morrow. Fear is a powerful emotion. People rarely think clearly, me included, when it consumes us.

Obviously, saying that securities might rise or drop is not much help. That's beside the point. The larger issue is

Concluding Remarks

solvency. An investor can hedge against a tail event like a dollar implosion by buying gold and silver. Or they can mock the rationale of gold and silver as do financial journalists, central bankers, mushy headed economists and the like.

In my book gold is freedom. Paper money is slavery.

Paper money is the scourge of dishonest government and men who want something for free, something that doesn't belong to them, something that rightly belongs to someone else but they want.

Kings, queens, dictators, tyrants and heirs of a once free republic have used paper money. These people have used paper money to peddle influence and wage wars that had little support, particularly if peace-loving people were given the choice between waging war through higher taxes and a greater debt load; or seeking a peaceful negotiation before storming off to war.

Free men have chosen gold when given the chance. Gold is honest money for honest men. There are no counterclaims to it. If you own gold, it's yours.

Summary

Gold is the money of free men because it is the most liquid commodity on the face of the earth, it is the best form of money and it is the most recognized money on the planet.

Gold is the money that the free market has chosen over the millennia because 1) gold is the most liquid commodity on the face of the earth 2) gold is the best form

Concluding Remarks

of money 3) gold is the most recognized money on the planet 4) gold has no counterclaims – if you own it, it's yours.

Where ever you go on earth gold opens doors. It speaks loudly to people about whom you are and what you represent.

Gold and Silver: Freedom and Liberty

Bibliography

Angell, Norman. *The Story of Money.* New York: Garden City Publishing, 1929.

Awalt, Francis G. *Recollections of the Banking Crisis in 1933, from a History of the Federal Reserve: Volume 1: 1913-1951.* St. Louis Federal Reserve. Business History Review, 43, autumn, 1969.

Badger, Anthony J., *FDR: The First Hundred Days.* New York: Hill and Wang, 2009.

Bruner, Robert F. and Sean D. Carr. *The Panic of 1907: Lessons Learned from the Market's Perfect Storm.* Hoboken, NJ: John Wiley & Sons, 2007.

Chernow, Ron. *The House of Morgan: An American Banking Dynasty and the Rise of Modern Finance.* New York: Atlantic Monthly Press, 1990.

Coinage Act of 1792.

Congressional Record, 77th Congress.

Constitution of the United States.

Crowley, Roger. *1453: The Holy War for Constantinople and The Clash of Islam and The West.* New York: Hyperion, 2005.

Ferguson, E. James. *The Power of the Purse: A History of American Public Finance, 1776-1790.* Chapel Hill: University of North Carolina Press, 1961.

Goodman, Martin. *Rome and Jerusalem: The Clash of Ancient Civilizations.* New York: Alfred A. Knopf, 2007.

Bibliography

Henry Hazlitt. *From Bretton Woods to World Inflation: A Study of Causes and Consequences* Chicago: Regnery Gateway, 2009.

Heather, Peter. *The Fall of the Roman Empire: A New History.* London: Pan Macmillan, 2006.

History of Herodotus, Volume 1. New York: E.P. Dutton, 1916.

Hodges, H. R. *Economic Conditions: 1815 – 1914.* London: George Allen & Unwin, 1917.

Jastram, Roy W. and Jill Leyland. The Golden Constant: The English and American Experience, 1560 - 2007. Northampton, MA. Edward Elgar, 2007.

Kemmerer, Edwin Walter. *Gold and the Gold Standard: The Story of Gold Money, Past Present and Future.* New York: McGraw-Hill Book Company, 1944.

Larson, Edward J. and Michael P. Winship. *The Constitutional Convention.* New York: The Modern Library, 2005.

Laughlin, J. Laurence. *The History of Bimetallism in the United States.* New York: D. Appleton and Co., 1898.

Kolko, Gabriel. *The Triumph of Conservatism: A Reinterpretation of American History, 1900-1916.* London: Free Press of Glen Collier-MacMillan, 1963.

Lips, Ferdinand. *Gold Wars: The Battle Against Sound Money as Seen From a Swiss Perspective.* New York: The Foundation for the Advancement of Monetary Education, 2001.

Bibliography

Paul, Ron and Lewis Lehrman. The Case for Gold. Auburn, Alabama: The Ludwig Von Mises Institute, 2007.

Rappleye, Charles. *Robert Morris.* New York: Simon and Schuster, 2010.

Romer, Christina D. *Journal of Economic Perspectives.* Volume 13, Number 2, Spring 1999.

Rothbard, Murray N. *A History of Money and Banking in the United States: The Colonial Era to WW II.* Auburn, Alabama: Ludwig von Mises Institute, 2002.

Rozeff, Michael S. *The U.S. Constitution and Money: Corruption and Decline.* The Writer's Free Internet Edition – Volume III. (East Amherst, 2010)

Scott, E. H. *Journal of the Federal Convention.* Chicago: Albert, Scott & Co., 1894. Cornell University Library. http://www.archive.org/details/cu31924009891684

Scott, James Brown. *James Madison's Notes of Debates in the Federal Convention of 1787 and their Relation to a More Perfect Society of Nations.* New York: Oxford University Press, 1918. (BiblioLife, LLC historical reproduction)

Selgin, George, William Lastrapes, Lawrence White, *"Has the Fed Been a Failure?" Cato Working Paper* Dec. 2010

Shlaes, Amity. *The Forgotten Man: A New History of the Great Depression.* New York: Harper Perennial, 2008.

St. Louis Federal Reserve Web Site.

Tullock, Gordon. *Paper Money: A Cycle in Cathay.* The Economic History Review, 1957.

Bibliography

Woods, Thomas and Kevin Gutzman. *Who Killed the Constitution?* New York: Crown Forum, 2008.

White, Horace. *Money and Banking.* Boston: Ginn and Co., 1902.

Appendix

The following information was provided courtesy of the St. Louis Federal Reserve, The Congressional Record and The American Presidency Project: Online by Gerhard Peters and John T. Woolley: http://www.presidency.ucsb.edu

FDR Proclamations and Fireside Chats

Proclamation 2038

March 5, 1933 Congressional Extra Session

By the President of the United States of America

A Proclamation

Whereas public interests require that the Congress of the United States should be convened in extra session at twelve o'clock, noon, on the Ninth day of March, 1933, to receive such communication as may be made by the Executive;

Now, Therefore, I, Franklin D. Roosevelt, President of the United States of America, do hereby proclaim and declare that an extraordinary occasion requires the Congress of the United States to convene in extra session at the Capitol in the City of Washington on the Ninth day of March, 1933, at twelve o'clock, noon, of which all persons who shall at that time be entitled to act as members thereof are hereby required to take notice.

In Witness Whereof, I have hereunto set my hand and caused to be affixed the great seal of the United States.

Franklin D. Roosevelt

Appendix

Citation: Franklin D. Roosevelt: "Proclamation 2038 - Calling Congress into Extraordinary Session," March 5, 1933. Online by Gerhard Peters and John T. Woolley, The American Presidency Project.

http://www.presidency.ucsb.edu/ws/?pid=14584

Appendix

Proclamation 2039

March 6, 1933 National Emergency Banking Holiday

Whereas there have been heavy and unwarranted withdrawals of gold and currency from our banking institutions for the purpose of hoarding; and

Whereas continuous and increasingly extensive speculative activity abroad in foreign exchange has resulted in severe drains on the Nation's stocks of gold; and

Whereas those conditions have created a national emergency; and

Whereas it is in the best interests of all bank depositors that a period of respite be provided with a view to preventing further hoarding of coin, bullion or currency or speculation in foreign exchange and permitting the application of appropriate measures to protect the interests of our people; and

Whereas it is provided in Section 5 (b) of the Act of October 6, 1917 (40 Stat. L. 411), as amended, "That the President may investigate, regulate, or prohibit, under such rules and regulations as he may prescribe, by means of licenses or otherwise, any transactions in foreign exchange and the export, hoarding, melting, or ear markings of gold or silver coin or bullion or currency . . ."; and

Whereas it is provided in Section 16 of the said Act "That whoever shall willfully violate any of the provisions of this Act or of any license, rule, or regulation issued thereunder, and whoever shall willfully violate, neglect, or refuse to comply with any order of the President issued in compliance

Appendix

with the provisions of this Act, shall, upon conviction, be fined not more than $10,000, or, if a natural person, imprisoned for not more than ten years, or both . . .";

Now, Therefore I, Franklin D. Roosevelt, President of the United States of America, in view of such national emergency and by virtue of the authority vested in me by said Act and in order to prevent the export, hoarding, or earmarking of gold or silver coin or bullion or currency, do hereby proclaim, order, direct and declare that from Monday, the Sixth day of March, to Thursday, the Ninth day of March, Nineteen Hundred and Thirty-three, both dates inclusive, there shall be maintained and observed by all banking institutions and all branches thereof located in the United States of America, including the territories and insular possessions, a bank holiday, and that during said period all banking transactions shall be suspended. During such holiday, excepting as hereinafter provided, no such banking institution or branch shall pay out, export, earmark, or permit the withdrawal or transfer in any manner or by any device whatsoever, of any gold or silver coin or bullion or currency or take any other action which might facilitate the hoarding thereof; nor shall any such banking institution or branch pay out deposits, make loans or discounts, deal in foreign exchange, transfer credits from the United States to any place abroad, or transact any other banking business whatsoever.

During such holiday, the Secretary of the Treasury, with the approval of the President and under such regulations as he may prescribe, is authorized and empowered (a) to permit any or all of such banking institutions to perform any or all of the usual banking functions, (b) to direct, require or permit the issuance of clearing house certificates or other

Appendix

evidences of claims against assets of banking institutions, and (c) to authorize and direct the creation in such banking institutions of special trust accounts for the receipt of new deposits which shall be subject to withdrawal on demand without any restriction or limitation and shall be kept separately in cash or on deposit in Federal Reserve Banks or invested in obligations of the United States.

As used in this order the term "banking institutions" shall include all Federal Reserve Banks, national banking associations, banks, trust companies, savings banks, building and loan associations, credit unions, or other corporations, partnerships, associations or persons, engaged in the business of receiving deposits, making loans, discounting business paper, or transacting any other form of banking business.

Franklin D. Roosevelt

Citation: Franklin D. Roosevelt: "Proclamation 2039 - Declaring Bank Holiday," March 6, 1933. Online by Gerhard Peters and John T. Woolley, The American Presidency Project. http://www.presidency.ucsb.edu/ws/?pid=14661.

Appendix

Proclamation 2040

Extending National Emergency

March 9, 1933

Whereas, on March 6, 1933, I, Franklin D. Roosevelt, President of the United States of America, by Proclamation declared the existence of a national emergency and proclaimed a bank holiday extending from Monday the 6th day of March to Thursday the 9th day of March, 1933, both dates inclusive, in order to prevent the export, hoarding or earmarking of gold or silver coin, or bullion or currency, or speculation in foreign exchange; and

Whereas, under the Act of March 9, 1933, all Proclamations heretofore or hereafter issued by the President pursuant to the authority conferred by section 5 (b) of the Act of October 6, 1917, as amended, are approved and confirmed; and

Whereas, said national emergency still continues, and it is necessary to take further measures extending beyond March 9, 1933, in order to accomplish such purposes:

Now, Therefore, I, Franklin D. Roosevelt, President of the United States of America, in view of such continuing national emergency and by virtue of the authority vested in me by Section 5 (b) of the Act of October 6, 1917 (40 Stat. L. 411), as amended by the Act of March 9, 1933, do hereby proclaim, order, direct and declare that all the terms and provisions of said Proclamation of March 6, 1933, and the regulations and orders issued thereunder are hereby continued in full force and effect until further proclamation by the President.

Appendix

In Witness Whereof, I have hereunto set my hand and have caused the seal of the United States to be affixed.

Done in the District of Columbia, this 9th day of March, in the Year of our Lord One Thousand Nine Hundred and Thirty three, and of the Independence of the United States the One Hundredth and Fifty-seventh.

Franklin D. Roosevelt

By the President: Cordell Hull, Secretary of State

Citation: Franklin D. Roosevelt: "Proclamation 2040 - Bank Holiday," March 9, 1933. Online by Gerhard Peters and John T. Woolley, The American Presidency Project. http://www.presidency.ucsb.edu/ws/?pid=14485.

Appendix

Executive Order 6073

Re-Opening the Banks

March 10, 1933

By Virtue of the authority vested in me by Section 5 (b) of the Act of October 6, 1917 (40 Stat. L., 411), as amended by the Act of March 9, 1933, and by Section 4 of the said Act of March 9, 1933, and by virtue of all other authority vested in me, I hereby issue the following executive order.

The Secretary of the Treasury is authorized and empowered under such regulations as he may prescribe to permit any member bank of the Federal Reserve System and any other banking institution organized under the laws of the United States, to perform any or all of their usual banking functions, except as otherwise prohibited.

The appropriate authority having immediate supervision of banking institutions in each State or any place subject to the jurisdiction of the United States is authorized and empowered under such regulations as such authority may prescribe to permit any banking institution in such State or place, other than banking institutions covered by the foregoing paragraph, to perform any or all of their usual banking functions, except as otherwise prohibited.

All banks which are members of the Federal Reserve System, desiring to reopen for the performance of all usual and normal banking functions, except as otherwise prohibited, shall apply for a license therefor to the Secretary of the Treasury. Such application shall be filed immediately through the Federal Reserve Banks. The Federal Reserve Bank shall then transmit such applications to the Secretary of

Appendix

the Treasury. Licenses will be issued by the Federal Reserve Bank upon approval of the Secretary of the Treasury. The Federal Reserve Banks are hereby designated as agents of the Secretary of the Treasury for the receiving of application and the issuance of licenses in his behalf and upon his instructions.

Until further order, no individual, partnership, association, or corporation, including any banking institution, shall export or otherwise remove or permit to be withdrawn from the United States or any place subject to the jurisdiction thereof any gold coin, gold bullion, or gold certificates, except in accordance with regulations prescribed by or under license issued by the Secretary of the Treasury.

No permission to any banking institution to perform any banking functions shall authorize such institution to pay out any gold coin, gold bullion or gold certificates except as authorized by the Secretary of the Treasury, nor to allow withdrawal of any currency for hoarding, nor to engage in any transaction in foreign exchange except such as may be undertaken for legitimate and normal business requirements, for reasonable traveling and other personal requirements, and for the fulfillment of contracts entered into prior to March 6, 1933.

Every Federal Reserve Bank is authorized and instructed to keep itself currently informed as to transactions in foreign exchange entered into or consummated within its district and shall report to the Secretary of the Treasury all transactions in foreign exchange which are prohibited.

Appendix

Citation: Franklin D. Roosevelt: "Executive Order 6073 - Reopening Banks," March 10, 1933. Online by Gerhard Peters and John T. Woolley, The American Presidency Project. http://www.presidency.ucsb.edu/ws/?pid=14507.

Appendix

FDR Banking Fireside Chat to American People

March 12, 1933

I want to talk for a few minutes with the people of the United States about banking—with the comparatively few who understand the mechanics of banking but more particularly with the overwhelming majority who use banks for the making of deposits and the drawing of checks. I want to tell you what has been done in the last few days, why it was done, and what the next steps are going to be. I recognize that the many proclamations from State capitols and from Washington, the legislation, the Treasury regulations, etc., couched for the most part in banking and legal terms, should be explained for the benefit of the average citizen. I owe this in particular because of the fortitude and good temper with which everybody has accepted the inconvenience and hardships of the banking holiday. I know that when you understand what we in Washington have been about I shall continue to have your cooperation as fully as I have had your sympathy and help during the past week.

First of all, let me state the simple fact that when you deposit money in a bank the bank does not put the money into a safe deposit vault. It invests your money in many different forms of credit—bonds, commercial paper, mortgages and many other kinds of loans. In other words, the bank puts your money to work to keep the wheels of industry and of agriculture turning around. A comparatively small part of the money you put into the bank is kept in currency—an amount which in normal times is wholly sufficient to cover the cash needs of the average citizen. In other words, the total amount of all the currency in the country is only a small fraction of the total deposits in all of the banks.

Appendix

What, then, happened during the last few days of February and the first few days of March? Because of undermined confidence on the part of the public, there was a general rush by a large portion of our population to turn bank deposits into currency or gold—a rush so great that the soundest banks could not get enough currency to meet the demand. The reason for this was that on the spur of the moment it was, of course, impossible to sell perfectly sound assets of a bank and convert them into cash except at panic prices far below their real value.

By the afternoon of March 3d scarcely a bank in the country was open to do business. Proclamations temporarily closing them in whole or in part had been issued by the Governors in almost all the States.

It was then that I issued the proclamation providing for the nationwide bank holiday, and this was the first step in the Government's reconstruction of our financial and economic fabric.

The second step was the legislation promptly and patriotically passed by the Congress confirming my proclamation and broadening my powers so that it became possible in view of the requirement of time to extend the holiday and lift the ban of that holiday gradually. This law also gave authority to develop a program of rehabilitation of our banking facilities. I want to tell our citizens in every part of the Nation that the national Congress—Republicans and Democrats alike—showed by this action a devotion to public welfare and a realization of the emergency and the necessity for speed that it is difficult to match in our history.

Appendix

The third stage has been the series of regulations permitting the banks to continue their functions to take care of the distribution of food and household necessities and the payment of payrolls.

This bank holiday, while resulting in many cases in great inconvenience, is affording us the opportunity to supply the currency necessary to meet the situation. No sound bank is a dollar worse off than it was when it closed its doors last Monday. Neither is any bank which may turn out not to be in a position for immediate opening. The new law allows the twelve Federal Reserve Banks to issue additional currency on good assets and thus the banks which reopen will be able to meet every legitimate call. The new currency is being sent out by the Bureau of Engraving and Printing in large volume to every part of the country. It is sound currency because it is backed by actual, good assets.

A question you will ask is this: why are all the banks not to be reopened at the same time? The answer is simple. Your Government does not intend that the history of the past few years shall be repeated. We do not want and will not have another epidemic of bank failures.

As a result, we start tomorrow, Monday, with the opening of banks in the twelve Federal Reserve Bank cities—those banks which on first examination by the Treasury have already been found to be all right. This will be followed on Tuesday by the resumption of all their functions by banks already found to be sound in cities where there are recognized clearing houses. That means about 250 cities of the United States.

Appendix

On Wednesday and succeeding days banks in smaller places all through the country will resume business, subject, of course, to the Government's physical ability to complete its survey. It is necessary that the reopening of banks be extended over a period in order to permit the banks to make applications for necessary loans, to obtain currency needed to meet their requirements and to enable the Government to make common sense checkups.

Let me make it clear to you that if your bank does not open the first day you are by no means justified in believing that it will not open. A bank that opens on one of the subsequent days is in exactly the same status as the bank that opens tomorrow.

I know that many people are worrying about State banks not members of the Federal Reserve System. These banks can and will receive assistance from member banks and from the Reconstruction Finance Corporation. These State banks are following the same course as the National banks except that they get their licenses to resume business from the State authorities, and these authorities have been asked by the Secretary of the Treasury to permit their good banks to open up on the same schedule as the national banks. I am confident that the State Banking Departments will be as careful as the national Government in the policy relating to the opening of banks and will follow the same broad policy.

It is possible that when the banks resume a very few people who have not recovered from their fear may again begin withdrawals. Let me make it clear that the banks will take care of all needs—and it is my belief that hoarding during the past week has become an exceedingly unfashionable pastime. It needs no prophet to tell you that when the people

Appendix

find that they can get their money— that they can get it when they want it for all legitimate purposes—the phantom of fear will soon be laid. People will again be glad to have their money where it will be safely taken care of and where they can use it conveniently at any time. I can assure you that it is safer to keep your money in a reopened bank than under the mattress.

The success of our whole great national program depends, of course, upon the cooperation of the public—on its intelligent support and use of a reliable system.

Remember that the essential accomplishment of the new legislation is that it makes it possible for banks more readily to convert their assets into cash than was the case before. More liberal provision has been made for banks to borrow on these assets at the Reserve Banks and more liberal provision has also been made for issuing currency on the security of these good assets. This currency is not fiat currency. It is issued only on adequate security, and every good bank has an abundance of such security.

One more point before I close. There will be, of course, some banks unable to reopen without being reorganized. The new law allows the Government to assist in making these reorganizations quickly and effectively and even allows the Government to subscribe to at least a part of new capital which may be required.

I hope you can see from this elemental recital of what your Government is doing that there is nothing complex, or radical, in the process.

We had a bad banking situation. Some of our bankers had shown themselves either incompetent or dishonest in their

Appendix

handling of the people's funds. They had used the money entrusted to them in speculations and unwise loans. This was, of course, not true in the vast majority of our banks, but it was true in enough of them to shock the people for a time into a sense of insecurity and to put them into a frame of mind where they did not differentiate, but seemed to assume that the acts of a comparative few had tainted them all. It was the Government's job to straighten out this situation and do it as quickly as possible. And the job is being performed.

I do not promise you that every bank will be reopened or that individual losses will not be suffered, but there will be no losses that possibly could be avoided; and there would have been more and greater losses had we continued to drift. I can even promise you salvation for some at least of the sorely pressed banks. We shall be engaged not merely in reopening sound banks but in the creation of sound banks through reorganization.

It has been wonderful to me to catch the note of confidence from all over the country. I can never be sufficiently grateful to the people for the loyal support they have given me in their acceptance of the judgment that has dictated our course, even though all our processes may not have seemed clear to them.

After all, there is an element in the readjustment of our financial system more important than currency, more important than gold, and that is the confidence of the people. Confidence and courage are the essentials of success in carrying out our plan. You people must have faith; you must not be stampeded by rumors or guesses. Let us unite in banishing fear. We have provided the machinery to restore

Appendix

our financial system; it is up to you to support and make it work.

It is your problem no less than it is mine. Together we cannot fail.

Citation: Franklin D. Roosevelt: "Fireside Chat on Banking," March 12, 1933. Online by Gerhard Peters and John T. Woolley, The American Presidency Project. http://www.presidency.ucsb.edu/ws/?pid=14540.

Appendix

Order for People to Turn in their Gold

April 6, 1933

FEDERAL RESERVE BANK OF ST. LOUIS

April 6, 1933.

PRESS STATEMENT

To All Banks in District No. 8:

The Secretary of the Treasury released the following statement to the Press on the late afternoon of April 5:

"The President's order of today requiring the turning in of hoarded gold, and at the same time providing that gold shall be available for all proper purposes, is an expected step in the process of regularizing our monetary position and furnishing adequate banking and currency facilities for all customary needs.

"Such an order was in contemplation from the time of the passage of the emergency banking act. As the President indicated today, while many of our citizens voluntarily and helpfully turned in their gold, there were others who did not so respond. In fairness, the conduct of all citizens with reference to gold should be the same in this emergency, and this is assured by the order.

Those surrendering gold, of course, receive an equivalent amount of other forms of currency, and other forms of currency may be used for obtaining gold in an equivalent amount where authorized for proper purposes.

"Gold held in private hoards serves no useful purpose under present circumstances; when added to the stock of the

Appendix

Federal Reserve banks it serves as a basis for currency and credit. This further strengthening of the banking structure adds to its power of service toward recovery.

"A vital provision of the order is that authorizing the Secretary of the Treasury to issue licenses for gold for proper business needs not involving hoarding. Applications will be passed upon as the facts in each case warrant.

"Regulations governing the procedure of the Treasury under the new order are in course of preparation."

Respectfully,

Wm. McC. Martin, Governor

Citation: St. Louis Federal Reserve

http://fraser.stlouisfed.org/docs/historical/frbsl_history/bank_holiday/pressstatement_19330406.pdf

Appendix

FDR Follow up Fireside Chat to the American People on Gold and Other Measures Undertaken since Inauguration

May 7, 1933

On A Sunday night a week after my Inauguration I used the radio to tell you about the banking crisis and the measures we were taking to meet it. I think that in that way I made clear to the country various facts that might otherwise have been misunderstood and in general provided a means of understanding which did much to restore confidence.

Tonight, eight weeks later, I come for the second time to give you my report; in the same spirit and by the same means to tell you about what we have been doing and what we are planning to do.

Two months ago we were facing serious problems. The country was dying by inches. It was dying because trade and commerce had declined to dangerously low levels; prices for basic commodities were such as to destroy the value of the assets of national institutions such as banks, savings banks, insurance companies, and others. These institutions, because of their great needs, were foreclosing mortgages, calling loans, refusing credit. Thus there was actually in process of destruction the property of millions of people, who had borrowed money on that property in terms of dollars which had had an entirely different value from the level of March, 1933. That situation in that crisis did not call for any complicated consideration of economic panaceas or fancy plans. We were faced by a condition and not a theory.

There were just two alternatives: The first was to allow the foreclosures to continue, credit to be withheld and money to

Appendix

go into hiding, thus forcing liquidation and bankruptcy of banks, railroads and insurance companies and a recapitalizing of all business and all property on a lower level. This alternative meant a continuation of what is loosely called "deflation," the net result of which would have been extraordinary hardships on all property owners and, incidentally, extraordinary hardships on all persons working for wages through an increase in unemployment and a further reduction of the wage scale.

It is easy to see that the result of this course would have not only economic effects of a very serious nature, but social results that might bring incalculable harm. Even before I was inaugurated I came to the conclusion that such a policy was too much to ask the American people to bear. It involved not only a further loss of homes, farms, savings and wages, but also a loss of spiritual values—the loss of that sense of security for the present and the future so necessary to the peace and contentment of the individual and of his family. When you destroy these things you will find it difficult to establish confidence of any sort in the future. It was clear that mere appeals from Washington for confidence and the mere lending of more money to shaky institutions could not stop this downward course. A prompt program applied as quickly as possible seemed to me not only justified but imperative to our national security. The Congress, and when I say Congress I mean the members of both political parties, fully understood this and gave me generous and intelligent support. The members of Congress realized that the methods of normal times had to be replaced in the emergency by measures which were suited to the serious and pressing requirements of the moment. There was no actual surrender of power, Congress still retained its constitutional authority,

Appendix

and no one has the slightest desire to change the balance of these powers. The function of Congress is to decide what has to be done and to select the appropriate agency to carry out its will. To this policy it has strictly adhered. The only thing that has been happening has been to designate the President as the agency to carry out certain of the purposes of the Congress. This was constitutional and in keeping with the past American tradition.

The legislation which has been passed or is in the process of enactment can properly be considered as part of a well-grounded plan.

First, we are giving opportunity of employment to one-quarter of a million of the unemployed, especially the young men who have dependents, to go into the forestry and flood-prevention work. This is a big task because it means feeding, clothing and caring for nearly twice as many men as we have in the regular army itself. In creating this civilian conservation corps we are killing two birds with one stone. We are clearly enhancing the value of our natural resources, and we are relieving an appreciable amount of actual distress. This great group of men has entered upon its work on a purely voluntary basis; no military training is involved and we are conserving not only our natural resources, but our human resources. One of the great values to this work is the fact that it is direct and requires the intervention of very little machinery.

Second, I have requested the Congress and have secured action upon a proposal to put the great properties owned by our Government at Muscle Shoals to work after long years of wasteful inaction, and with this a broad plan for the improvement of a vast area in the Tennessee Valley. It will

Appendix

add to the comfort and happiness of hundreds of thousands of people and the incident benefits will reach the entire Nation.

Next, the Congress is about to pass legislation that will greatly ease the mortgage distress among the farmers and the home owners of the Nation, by providing for the easing of the burden of debt now bearing so heavily upon millions of our people.

Our next step in seeking immediate relief is a grant of half a billion dollars to help the States, counties and municipalities in their duty to care for those who need direct and immediate relief.

The Congress also passed legislation authorizing the sale of beer in such States as desired it. This has already resulted in considerable reemployment and incidentally has provided much needed tax revenue.

We are planning to ask the Congress for legislation to enable the Government to undertake public works, thus stimulating directly and indirectly the employment of many others in well-considered projects.

Further legislation has been taken up which goes much more fundamentally into our economic problems. The Farm Relief Bill seeks by the use of several methods, alone or together, to bring about an increased return to farmers for their major farm products, seeking at the same time to prevent in the days to come disastrous overproduction which so often in the past has kept farm commodity prices far below a reasonable return. This measure provides wide powers for emergencies. The extent of its use will depend entirely upon what the future has in store.

Appendix

Well-considered and conservative measures will likewise be proposed which will attempt to give to the industrial workers of the country a more fair wage return, prevent cut-throat competition and unduly long hours for labor, and at the same time encourage each industry to prevent overproduction.

Our Railroad Bill falls into the same class because it seeks to provide and make certain definite planning by the railroads themselves, with the assistance of the Government, to eliminate the duplication and waste that is now resulting in railroad receiverships and continuing operating deficits.

I am certain that the people of this country understand and approve the broad purposes behind these new governmental policies relating to agriculture and industry and transportation. We found ourselves faced with more agricultural products than we could possibly consume ourselves and with surpluses which other Nations did not have the cash to buy from us except at prices ruinously low. We found our factories able to turn out more goods than we could possibly consume, and at the same time we were faced with a falling export demand. We found ourselves with more facilities to transport goods and crops than there were goods and crops to be transported. All of this has been caused in large part by a complete lack of planning and a complete failure to understand the danger signals that have been flying ever since the close of the World War. The people of this country have been erroneously encouraged to believe that they could keep on increasing the output of farm and factory indefinitely and that some magician would find ways and means for that increased output to be consumed with reasonable profit to the producer.

Appendix

Today we have reason to believe that things are a little better than they were two months ago. Industry has picked up, railroads are carrying more freight, farm prices are better, but I am not going to indulge in issuing proclamations of overenthusiastic assurance. We cannot ballyhoo ourselves back to prosperity. I am going to be honest at all times with the people of the country. I do not want the people of this country to take the foolish course of letting this improvement come back on another speculative wave. I do not want the people to believe that because of unjustified optimism we can resume the ruinous practice of increasing our crop output and our factory output in the hope that a kind Providence will find buyers at high prices. Such a course may bring us immediate and false prosperity but it will be the kind of prosperity that will lead us into another tailspin.

It is wholly wrong to call the measures that we have taken Government control of farming, industry, and transportation. It is rather a partnership between Government and farming and industry and transportation, not partnership in profits, for the profits still go to the citizens, but rather a partnership in planning, and a partnership to see that the plans are carried out.

Let me illustrate with an example. Take the cotton-goods industry. It is probably true that 90 percent of the cotton manufacturers would agree to eliminate starvation wages, would agree to stop long hours of employment, would agree to stop child labor, would agree to prevent an overproduction that would result in unsalable surpluses. But, what good is such an agreement if the other 10 percent of cotton manufacturers pay starvation wages, require long hours, employ children in their mills and turn out burdensome surpluses? The unfair 10 percent could produce goods so

Appendix

cheaply that the fair 90 percent would be compelled to meet the unfair conditions. Here is where Government comes in. Government ought to have the right and will have the right, after surveying and planning for an industry, to prevent, with the assistance of the overwhelming majority of that industry, unfair practices and to enforce this agreement by the authority of Government. The so-called anti-trust laws were intended to prevent the creation of monopolies and to forbid unreasonable profits to those monopolies. That purpose of the antitrust laws must be continued, but these laws were never intended to encourage the kind of unfair competition that results in long hours, starvation wages and overproduction.

The same principle applies to farm products and to transportation and every other field of organized private industry.

We are working toward a definite goal, which is to prevent the return of conditions which came very close to destroying what we call modern civilization. The actual accomplishment of our purpose cannot be attained in a day. Our policies are wholly within purposes for which our American Constitutional Government was established 150 years ago.

I know that the people of this country will understand this and will also understand the spirit in which we are undertaking this policy. I do not deny that we may make mistakes of procedure as we carry out the policy. I have no expectation of making a hit every time I come to bat. What I seek is the highest possible batting average, not only for myself but for the team. Theodore Roosevelt once said to

Appendix

me: "If I can be right 75 percent of the time I shall come up to the fullest measure of my hopes."

Much has been said of late about Federal finances and inflation, the gold standard, etc. Let me make the facts very simple and my policy very clear. In the first place, Government credit and Government currency is really one and the same thing. Behind Government bonds there is only a promise to pay. Behind Government currency we have, in addition to the promise to pay, a reserve of gold and a small reserve of silver. In this connection it is worthwhile remembering that in the past the Government has agreed to redeem nearly thirty billions of its debts and its currency in gold, and private corporations in this country have agreed to redeem another sixty or seventy billions of securities and mortgages in gold. The Government and private corporations were making these agreements when they knew full well that all of the gold in the United States amounted to only between three and four billions and that all of the gold in all of the world amounted to only about eleven billions.

If the holders of these promises to pay started in to demand gold the first comers would get gold for a few days and they would amount to about one-twenty-fifth of the holders of the securities and the currency. The other twenty-four people out of twenty-five, who did not happen to be at the top of the line, would be told politely that there was no more gold left. We have decided to treat all twenty-five in the same way in the interest of justice and the exercise of the constitutional powers of this Government. We have placed everyone on the same basis in order that the general good may be preserved.

Appendix

Nevertheless, gold, and to a partial extent silver, are perfectly good bases for currency, and that is why I decided not to let any of the gold now in the country go out of it.

A series of conditions arose three weeks ago which very readily might have meant, first, a drain on our gold by foreign countries, and second, as a result of that, a flight of American capital, in the form of gold, out of our country. It is not exaggerating the possibility to tell you that such an occurrence might well have taken from us the major part of our gold reserve and resulted in such a further weakening of our Government and private credit as to bring on actual panic conditions and the complete stoppage of the wheels of industry.

The Administration has the definite objective of raising commodity prices to such an extent that those who have borrowed money will, on the average, be able to repay that money in the same kind of dollar which they borrowed. We do not seek to let them get such a cheap dollar that they will be able to pay back a great deal less than they borrowed. In other words, we seek to correct a wrong and not to create another wrong in the opposite direction. That is why powers are being given to the Administration to provide, if necessary, for an enlargement of credit, in order to correct the existing wrong. These powers will be used when, as, and if it may be necessary to accomplish the purpose.

Hand in hand with the domestic situation which, of course, is our first concern is the world situation and I want to emphasize to you that the domestic situation is inevitably and deeply tied in with the conditions in all of the other Nations of the world. In other words, we can get, in all probability, a fair measure of prosperity to return in the

Appendix

United States, but it will not be permanent unless we get a return to prosperity all over the world.

In the conferences which we have held and are holding with the leaders of other Nations, we are seeking four great objectives: first, a general reduction of armaments and through this the removal of the fear of invasion and armed attack, and, at the same time, a reduction in armament costs, in order to help in the balancing of Government budgets and the reduction of taxation; second, a cutting down of the trade barriers, in order to restart the flow of exchange of crops and goods between Nations; third, the setting up of a stabilization of currencies, in order that trade can make contracts ahead; fourth, the reestablishment of friendly relations and greater confidence between all Nations.

Our foreign visitors these past three weeks have responded to these purposes in a very helpful way. All of the Nations have suffered alike in this great depression. They have all reached the conclusion that each can best be helped by the common action of all. It is in this spirit that our visitors have met with us and discussed our common problems. The international conference that lies before us must succeed. The future of the world demands it and we have each of us pledged ourselves to the best joint efforts to this end.

To you, the people of this country, all of us, the members of the Congress and the members of this Administration, owe a profound debt of gratitude. Throughout the depression you have been patient. You have granted us wide powers; you have encouraged us with a widespread approval of our purposes. Every ounce of strength and every resource at our command we have devoted to the end of justifying your confidence. We are encouraged to believe that a wise and

Appendix

sensible beginning has been made. In the present spirit of mutual confidence and mutual encouragement we go forward.

Citation: Franklin D. Roosevelt: "Second Fireside Chat." May 7, 1933. Online by Gerhard Peters and John T. Woolley, The American Presidency Project.

http://www.presidency.ucsb.edu/ws/?pid=14636.

Appendix

FDR Message to Senate and House during Extra Session

March 9, 1933

To the Senate and House of Representatives:

On March 3 banking operations in the United States ceased. To review at this time the causes of this failure of our banking system is unnecessary. Suffice it to say that the Government has been compelled to step in for the protection of depositors and the business of the Nation.

Our first task is to reopen all sound banks. This is an essential preliminary to subsequent legislation directed against speculation with the funds of depositors and other violations of positions of trust.

In order that the first objective-the opening of banks for the resumption of business-may be accomplished, I ask of the Congress the immediate enactment of legislation giving to the executive branch of the Government control over banks for the protection of depositors; authority forthwith to open such banks as have already been ascertained to be in sound condition, and other such banks, as rapidly as possible; and authority to reorganize and reopen such banks as may be found to require reorganization to put them on a sound basis.

I ask amendments to the Federal Reserve Act to provide for such additional currency, adequately secured, as it may become necessary to issue to meet all demands for currency and at the same time to achieve this end without increasing the unsecured indebtedness of the Government of the United States.

Appendix

I cannot too strongly urge upon the Congress the clear necessity for immediate action. A continuation of the strangulation of banking facilities is unthinkable. The passage of the proposed legislation will end this condition and, I trust, within a short space of time will result in a resumption of business activities.

In addition, it is my belief that this legislation will not only lift immediately all unwarranted doubts and suspicions in regard to banks which are 100 percent sound but will also mark the beginning of a new relationship between the banks and the people of this country.

The Members of the new Congress will realize, I am confident, the grave responsibility which lies upon me and upon them.

In the short space of 5 days it is impossible for us to formulate completed measures to prevent the recurrence of the evils of the past. This does not and should not, however, justify any delay in accomplishing this first step.

At an early moment I shall request of the Congress two other measures which I regard as of immediate urgency. With action taken thereon we can proceed to the consideration of a rounded program of national restoration.

Franklin D. Roosevelt.

The White House, March 9, 1933

Citation: Hein online: 73 Congress, First Session. Congressional Record. Pages 35/36.

http://unmasker4maine.files.wordpress.com/2011/01/janet-1933-march_9th-77congrec41.pdf.

Appendix

FDR Executive Order 6102

Mandate Gold Be Turned Over To Government

April 5, 1933

By virtue of the authority vested in me by Section 5 (b) of the Act of October 6, 1917, as amended by Section 2 of the Act of March 9, 1933, entitled "An Act to provide relief in the existing national emergency in banking, and for other purposes," in which amendatory Act Congress declared that a serious emergency exists, I, Franklin D. Roosevelt, President of the United States of America, do declare that said national emergency still continues to exist and pursuant to said section do hereby prohibit the hoarding of gold coin, gold bullion, and gold certificates within the continental United States by individuals, partnerships, associations and corporations and hereby prescribe the following regulations for carrying out the purposes of this order:

Section 1. For the purposes of this regulation, the term "hoarding" means the withdrawal and withholding of gold coin, gold bullion or gold certificates from the recognized and customary channels of trade. The term "person" means any individual, partnership, association or corporation.

Section 2. All persons are hereby required to deliver on or before May 1, 1933, to a Federal Reserve Bank or a branch or agency thereof or to any member bank of the Federal Reserve System all gold coin, gold bullion and gold certificates now owned by them or coming into their ownership on or before April 28, 1933, except the following:

(a) Such amount of gold as may be required for legitimate and customary use in industry, profession or art within a

Appendix

reasonable time, including gold prior to refining and stocks of gold in reasonable amounts for the usual trade requirements of owners mining and refining such gold.

(b) Gold coin and gold certificates in an amount not exceeding in the aggregate $100 belonging to any one person; and gold coins having a recognized special value to collectors of rare and unusual coins.

(c) Gold coin and bullion earmarked or held in trust for a recognized foreign Government or foreign central bank or the Bank for International Settlements.

(d) Gold coin and bullion licensed for other proper transactions (not involving hoarding) including gold coin and bullion imported for re-export or held pending action on applications for export licenses.

Section 3. Until otherwise ordered any person becoming the owner of any gold coin, gold bullion, or gold certificates after April 28, 1933, shall, within three days after receipt thereof, deliver the same in the manner prescribed in Section 2; unless such gold coin, gold bullion or gold certificates are held for any of the purposes specified in paragraphs (a), (b), or (c) of Section 2; or unless such gold coin or gold bullion is held for purposes specified in paragraph (d) of Section 2 and the person holding it is, with respect to such gold coin or bullion, a licensee or applicant for license pending action thereon.

Section 4. Upon receipt of gold coin, gold bullion or gold certificates delivered to it in accordance with Sections 2 or 3, the Federal Reserve Bank or member bank will pay therefor an equivalent amount of any other form of coin or currency coined or issued under the laws of the United States.

Appendix

Section 5. Member banks shall deliver all gold coin, gold bullion and gold certificates owned or received by them (other than as exempted under the provisions of Section 2) to the Federal Reserve Banks of their respective districts and receive credit or payment therefor.

Section 6. The Secretary of the Treasury, out of the sum made available to the President by Section 501 of the Act of March 9, 1933, will in all proper cases pay the reasonable costs of transportation of gold coin, gold bullion or gold certificates delivered to a member bank or Federal Reserve Bank in accordance with Section 2, 3, or 5 hereof, including the cost of insurance, protection, and such other incidental costs as may be necessary, upon production of satisfactory evidence of such costs. Voucher forms for this purpose may be procured from Federal Reserve Banks.

Section 7. In cases where the delivery of gold coin, gold bullion or gold certificates by the owners thereof within the time set forth above will involve extraordinary hardship or difficulty, the Secretary of the Treasury may, in his discretion, extend the time within which such delivery must be made. Applications for such extensions must be made in writing under oath, addressed to the Secretary of the Treasury and filed with a Federal Reserve Bank. Each application must state the date to which the extension is desired, the amount and location of the gold coin, gold bullion and gold certificates in respect of which such application is made and the facts showing extension to be necessary to avoid extraordinary hardship or difficulty.

Section 8. The Secretary of the Treasury is hereby authorized and empowered to issue such further regulations as he may deem necessary to carry out the purposes of this order and to

Appendix

issue licenses thereunder, through such officers or agencies as he may designate, including licenses permitting the Federal Reserve Banks and member banks of the Federal Reserve System, in return for an equivalent amount of other coin, currency or credit, to deliver, earmark or hold in trust gold coin and bullion to or for persons showing the need for the same for any of the purposes specified in paragraphs (a), (c) and (d) of Section 2 of these regulations.

Section 9. Whoever willfully violates any provision of this Executive Order or of these regulations or of any rule, regulation or license issued thereunder may be fined not more than $10,000, or, if a natural person, may be imprisoned for not more than ten years, or both; and any officer, director, or agent of any corporation who knowingly participates in any such violation may be punished by a like fine, imprisonment, or both.

This order and these regulations may be modified or revoked at any time.

Franklin D. Roosevelt

The White House, April 5, 1933.

Citation: Franklin D. Roosevelt: "Executive Order 6102 - Requiring Gold Coin, Gold Bullion and Gold Certificates to Be Delivered to the Government," April 5, 1933. Online by Gerhard Peters and John T. Woolley, The American Presidency Project.

http://www.presidency.ucsb.edu/ws/?pid=14611.

Index

A

Aldrich, Nelson, 69
Alexander the Great, 11
Aristotle, 2

B

banking holiday, 85
Barney, Charles, 68
Battle of Manzikert, 9
benefit of a gold coin standard, 57
bills of credit, 20
bimetallism, 42
brains trust, 92
Bretton Woods Agreement, 107
Britain, 11
British colonial policy, 25
British Sovereign., 12
Byzantium, 8

C

cartels, 64
Charles II, 16
Chase, Salmon, 49
China, 17
Coinage Act of 1792, 1
Competitive devaluations, 56
Confederate dollar, 40
Continental, 32
Croesus, 5
Currency Act, 28

D

default, defined, 80
deflation, 75
democrat platform of 1932, 81

Dinar, 9

E

Egyptians, 4
elastic currency, 70
electrum, 4
Emergency Banking Relief Act, 102
Executive Order 6073, 102
Executive Order 6102, 97
Executive Order 6260, 99

F

Fed performance review, 72
Federal Reserve, 70
Florin, 10
French and Indian War, 28

G

Genoa Conference in 1922, 53
globalism, 73
gold coin standard, 57
gold coin standard explained, 57
gold eagle, 45, 61
gold exchange standard, 52
Greeks, 5
Greenback, 40
Gresham's Law, 22, 30, 46, 47, 50, 57

H

Hamilton, Alexander, 42
Hoover, Herbert, 81

Index

I

IOU's, 21

J

Jefferson, Thomas, 62, 120

K

Knickerbocker Trust, 68

L

laissez-faire, 63
Locke, John, 99
London Gold Pool, 110
Lydians, 4

M

Madison, James, 40
Massachusetts Bay Mint Act, 15
Morris, Gouverneur, 43

N

National Monetary Commission, 69
Nero, 8
New Deal, 81
Nixon shock, 114

P

Papiermark, 40
Philip of Macedon, 11
Phoenicians, 11
pirates, 16
Ponzi scheme, 54
Proclamation 2039, 102
progressive legislation, 62

R

regulatory capture, 65
Reichsmark, 41
Rhode Island, 26, 27, 28
Rich Man's Panic of 1907, 66
Romans, 7

S

Sherman Antitrust Act, 64
Sherman, Roger, 43, 44
silver dollar, 44
small pox, 19, 37
Smithsonian Agreement, 115
Solidus, 8
specie, 14
Specie Resumption Act of 1875, 51

T

tobacco, 15
Trading with the Enemy Act of 1917, 86
traitorous gold hoarding, 85

V

Venetian Ducat, 10

W

War of 1812, 48
Warehouse receipts, 15
Washington, George, 36

About the Author

Bill Cross is an award winning Financial Consultant, Money Manager and stock trader. He has served as an Investment Consultant for Fortune 500 financial organizations, and as a Money Manager for a mutual fund. His brokerage licenses have included Series 3, 7, 8, 63 and 65. Mr. Cross has been in the financial services business since 1983. During his career Mr. Cross has managed six stockbrokerage offices, and has hired and trained a noteworthy number of new Investment Consultants. He attended the University of Texas, has a degree in Finance from the University of Houston at Clear Lake and a Master's degree in Business Administration from the University of St. Thomas. Mr. Cross was born and raised in Houston, Texas where he lives with his wife, Hazel, and daughter, Molly Margaret. He enjoys running marathons and swimming.

Made in the USA
Coppell, TX
08 November 2021